Emotionally Responsive Practice

Emotionally Responsive Practice

A Path for Schools That Heal Infancy-Grade 6

Lesley Koplow

TEACHERS COLLEGE PRESS

TEACHERS COLLEGE | COLUMBIA UNIVERSITY
NEW YORK AND LONDON

Published by Teachers College Press,® 1234 Amsterdam Avenue, New York, NY 10027

Library of Congress Cataloging-in-Publication Data

Names: Koplow, Lesley, author.
Title: Emotionally responsive practice : a path for schools that heal infancy-grade 6 / Lesley Koplow.
Description: New York, NY : Teachers College Press, [2021] | Includes bibliographical references and index.
Identifiers: LCCN 2020046558 (print) | LCCN 2020046559 (ebook) | ISBN 9780807764848 (paperback) | ISBN 9780807764855 (hardcover) | ISBN 9780807779316 (ebook)
Subjects: LCSH: Affective education. | Social learning—Study and teaching (Early childhood) | Social learning—Study and teaching (Elementary) | Emotional intelligence—Study and teaching (Early childhood) | Emotional intelligence—Study and teaching (Elementary)
Classification: LCC LB1072 .K72 2021 (print) | LCC LB1072 (ebook) | DDC 370.15/34—dc23
LC record available at https://lccn.loc.gov/2020046558
LC ebook record available at https://lccn.loc.gov/2020046559

ISBN 978-0-8077-6484-8 (paper)
ISBN 978-0-8077-6485-5 (hardcover)
ISBN 978-0-8077-7931-6 (ebook)

Printed on acid-free paper
Manufactured in the United States of America

Contents

Contents

Acknowledgments

I am grateful for Clara Lucia Campoli's assistance with formatting, and for the input of my talented colleagues at Bank Street, Margaret Blachly, Noelle Dean, Rachel Hass, Leslie Gartrell, Eva Peck, and Felice Wagman. I also want to acknowledge the work of teachers and school leaders who implement ERP, and who shared their experiences with me to inform my writing.

Preface

Once upon a time, teachers and school leaders who were passionate about their professional art took their freedom to practice authentically and creatively for granted. Now, in the age of standardization, that freedom is rare, won only through professional and parental activism and advocacy (Ravitch, 2020). Bringing the professional freedoms of the past together with the professional knowledge base of the present can empower schools to envision, fight for, and become stronger healing forces in the lives of the children and adults who are desperately looking for emotional connection and meaningful mastery in their days at school.

This preface is being written during the period of school closure brought about by COVID-19. Millions of children are sequestered in their homes, watching their teachers on a computer screen. Some children can make sense of this modality. Some cannot. Young children are wondering how their teachers got into those little Zoom rectangles, and why they can't come out.

Meanwhile, teachers are seeing and hearing the backgrounds that tell the stories of the children's lives. Some children are surrounded by age-appropriate toys, art materials, and comfortable working and living spaces. Their parents attempt to assist with confusing assignments or uncooperative technology. Other children sit in overcrowded spaces surrounded by household necessities, ambient noise, and a stressed parent or babysitter who is coping with a crying infant, a sick and quarantined grandparent, and a lack of nourishing food. Still others are invisible, at home without access to technology.

These images provide a new window into the life stories that children bring to school. All classroom teachers bear witness to the array of experiences that children have had, as these life stories play out in the classroom, emerging in interaction patterns, drawings, writing themes, play, and behavior that appear to come out of nowhere. Yet, the visual images in the Zoom windows are like illustrations of the stories that teachers have pieced together and have seen enacted within their classrooms when school is in session. When teachers observe their classrooms through the

Zoom lens, the socioeconomic and racial inequities that determine the day-to-day experiences of their children become glaringly obvious.

By and large, teachers are taught to ignore these disconcerting realities and to focus on the curricular expectations of their school or district. If children don't do well, often teacher motivation, parental commitment, and the child's own will to achieve are called into question.

Children may be referred for evaluation. Teachers may be rated as unsatisfactory. But in Schools That Heal, educators know that these measures don't address the core issues that make classroom life complicated for so many children.

Schools may not have the power to change the political forces that underly those issues, but they do have the ability to acknowledge children's real experiences in respectful and developmentally salient ways. They do have the responsibility to partner with children in "holding their stories" and making sure that children do not feel alone with, and distracted by, difficult experiences or unmet needs while they are in the classroom.

This book focuses on introducing readers to the core concepts and techniques of Emotionally Responsive Practice (ERP), which is a Social–Emotional Learning (SEL) approach that is used in collaboration with school communities seeking to support children, teachers, and parents. ERP classrooms are learning communities where children can see themselves reflected positively in their teacher's eyes, can find themselves in the curriculum, and can use literacy, social studies, and art as avenues for self-expression and integration of their own life experiences. Unlike many SEL programs, ERP does not focus on shaping behavior, legislating kindness, or reminding children to remain calm and positive, even as storm clouds gather. In ERP classrooms, teachers are not police officers, cheerleaders, or script readers, but are partners in development for the children in their communities.

When school districts decide that the control of COVID-19 in their area is such that children can come back to school, many will be carrying multiple losses and coping with life-altering changes. If we ignore these, the children who are in the most vulnerable situations will not thrive. Perhaps the extreme nature of our collective situation during the pandemic period will finally give educators permission to focus on the felt needs of children. If so, they will find that meeting the social and emotional needs of schoolchildren can create the cognitive, social, and emotional infrastructure that ultimately allows great expectations to be realized.

Emotionally Responsive Practice: A Path for Schools That Heal will guide educators toward a way of understanding and responding to disruptive circumstances and their social and emotional impact. The chapters in this book are grouped into three main parts. The first chapter of Part I looks at our public schools within a historical context. It examines how schools developed and changed in concert with the dominant social mores and political will of the times. In the current school climate, passionate educators often find themselves "swimming against a score-driven tide." Therefore, it becomes important to explore the origins of that tide, and to acknowledge the interaction between educational policy that undermines social and emotional well-being in schoolchildren, and the urgent need for social and emotional support in our schools. Chapters 2 and 3 present the conceptual foundations of ERP. These chapters introduce and elaborate on the lens of child development and the lens of children's life experiences as two essential and integral components of facilitating social and emotional health in school.

Part II of this book includes three chapters that give readers access to ERP techniques that can be integrated into classroom practice to support children who are struggling as well as those who are thriving. These techniques, including trauma-informed care, are meant to be implemented universally to avoid creating a distinction between happy kids and angry kids, or between kids who behave well and kids who do not within school community. ERP-informed schools know that sorting kids into categories of "good and bad" creates a gulf that gets wider and deeper as children grow and increases the risk of dangerous outcomes for all children.

Finally, the chapters in Part III look at the connection between creating multiple avenues of self-expression for both children and teachers within the school environment and the emotional well-being of school community. These chapters explore the process of developing symbols and metaphor as powerful tools for emotional integration.

In summary, this book is for the teachers, school leaders, school social workers, and parent and community advocates who care deeply about children, and want to connect with others whose inside stories of public education respect the emotional truth about teaching and learning in our time.

Part I

THE SMALLEST CIRCLE, THE BIGGEST UMBRELLA

CHAPTER 1

The Promise of Public Education

Emerging from a Checkered Past

Children live in a very small circle of relationships. This circle typically includes family members, neighbors, religious congregations for some, and the members of their school communities. Since the circle is small, each of these components makes a long-lasting contribution to children's emergent sense of self, safety, and well-being. Given the enormous variation in socioeconomic resources available to families and to neighborhoods in the United States and the current prevalence of social and emotional vulnerability among schoolchildren, public schools may be the umbrella with the most potential to protect both cognitive and emotional development for hundreds of thousands of children whose access to other resources may be limited.

LEARNING IN TIME: HISTORY, POLITICS, EDUCATION, AND CHILD MENTAL HEALTH

The notion that public school is the great equalizer for the children who attend is not unfamiliar. Recent education laws requiring U.S. public schools to use the Common Core State Standards (National Governors Association for Best Practice, 2010) to inform educational practice is perhaps motivated by the premise that if all children are exposed to similar curricula with the same standards, outcomes will improve across the economic spectrum. Although this approach has yet to yield that result, many public schools feel constrained by the requirements to meet these Common Core Standards, especially when the uniformity of demand does not take into account the variations in experiential knowledge that children bring to school. Indeed, a recent comprehensive study on the achievement gap showed school-community-poverty level to be the most salient factor responsible for the gap, including the impact of poverty of experience (Reardon et al., 2020).

In Emotionally Responsive Practice terms, the "common core" that must inform practice are the shared developmental interests, motivations, experiences, and symbols that allow children to engage fully and find meaning in their schoolwork. Emotionally Responsive Practice is based on the belief that schools can support the social and emotional infrastructure of cognitive development by appreciating and addressing the whole child's developmental issues and by communicating respect for their experiences. Therefore, it may be helpful to look at public schools in a historical light to find precedent for this kind of child-focused public school practice. In order to explore the promise of public schools to address *this* version of "common core," we look to history to understand how, when, and why these ingredients have been considered integral to public education or considered antithetical to it.

Education and Societal Purpose

The purpose of public education has evolved since the beginning of American history and has changed in concert with social ideals, sources of economic sustenance, and political tides. The ancestors of American public schools were the colonial "common schools" of the 17th century that required the "new world" born children of colonists to receive a basic literacy curriculum in service of furthering religious study and strengthening religious identity. Discipline was rigid, and emotional support was not on the agenda.

Formal academic education for its own sake was not a priority for the colonial agricultural economy. Indeed, formal public education did not begin to become a priority for the developing nation until the 1800s. Although Massachusetts and New York were the first states to require public elementary school attendance in 1852 and 1853, the country as a whole did not require it until 1918, or provide for public secondary education on a large scale until well into the 20th century (Mondale & Patton, 2001). One of the reasons for this slow rollout was the economic and racial stratification that was pervasive during the 18th and 19th centuries. Slaves and their children were intentionally denied education in an effort to keep them powerless. Wealthy people had their children taught at home, so they didn't feel a need for public education. Working-class families often depended on their children's labor to earn the meager incomes that would help their families to stay afloat.

As late as the 1930s, children beyond elementary school were expected to work. There were so many impoverished American children working in factories, service, and other industries at that time, that labor unions went to court to fight for child labor laws, arguing that children were taking jobs from adults during the Great Depression when jobs were scarce (Mondale & Patton, 2001). It was not until 1938 that nation-wide labor laws actually prevented employers from hiring children under 16 years old. When nationwide child labor laws went into effect, states gradually made school attendance compulsory from elementary school through the middle of high school (Mondale & Patton, 2001).

By 1918, all American children were required to attend elementary school, but public school attendance meant very different things to different populations of American children. Public education was highly segregated. Black children in the South were taught in separate facilities by law. Black teachers staffed these schools, many of whom were well qualified but forced to teach in dilapidated buildings with outdated books and minimal supplies (Mondale & Patton, 2001). The myth of separate but equal meant learning in freezing inadequate structures without access to resources. For Mexican children in the Southwest, it meant learning in separate classrooms or separate facilities with inexperienced teachers who were required to punish children for speaking Spanish and to encourage older children to learn a trade instead of staying in school. For Native American children, it meant being forcibly removed from parents to at-tend government-sponsored Christian boarding schools, whose mission was to erase the native child's cultural identity by any means possible, including abuse and starvation (Wong, 2019).

In 1954, the well-known Supreme Court case *Brown v. the Board of Education* struck down the Topeka, Kansas, lower court's decision up-holding the doctrine of separate but equal and ruled that segregation on the basis of race was unconstitutional. Chief Justice Earl Warren ruled that racial segregation "instilled a sense of inferiority that had a hugely detri-mental effect on the education and personal growth of African American children." However, authorities did not uniformly enforce this legal de-cision, leaving southern states to practice separate but equal education until 1968 when the civil rights movement fought to bring an end to the practice of educational segregation in the South.

When court-ordered busing was instituted in the late 1960s and early 1970s, and children of color were integrated into white southern schools, the newly integrated schools refused to hire teachers of color, leaving the former teachers of segregated schools without jobs, and the children of color without teachers who knew them well (Mondale & Patton, 2001). Meanwhile, federally sponsored housing discrimina-tion throughout the country continued to keep the majority of neigh-borhoods segregated, since the preponderance of American children attended their neighborhood schools. Although federal housing laws have since changed, de facto segregation continues to prevail in American schools today.

It was not until 1978, when the Indian Child Welfare Act was passed, that Native parents were allowed to refuse boarding school placement, although by that time, most of these institutions had already closed (Wong, 2019).

The history of public schools reveals a systematic effort to actively deny American children of color access to a high-quality school experience. Not only did schools neglect to support social and emotional development as it was understood at the time but worked to diminish children's mental health outcomes by engaging in abusive and demeaning treatment of the children they were charged with educating. In addition, since knowledge is power, children of color were steered away from academic studies as they grew older and counseled into vocational education.

An Early Wave of Immigration and a New Vision for Public Education

With the industrial revolution at the beginning of the 20th century came a wave of European immigrants eager for employment. Public schools were considered vehicles of enculturation for hundreds and thousands of children of immigrants. Those immigrant families who had enough resources to keep their children out of the workforce considered access to public education a bridge to the American Dream. Children were initially forbidden to speak their native languages in public schools, which created an unwelcoming sink-or-swim educational experience for many. Nevertheless, public school attendance made European immigrant parents hopeful about their children's futures.

Thirty-nine years before public education became compulsory in the United States, philosopher, educator, and author John Dewey developed an educational vision that differed radically from prior educational approaches. He and his colleagues at the University of Chicago wrote and taught a developmentally informed educational perspective that considered the minds of children as working differently than the minds of adults. Dewey had a deep belief that learning through life experience was the most meaningful form of education. He held that the process of learning within a social milieu through shared experiences helped to create the social fabric of a democratic society (Dewey, 1916/2015). Therefore, Dewey concluded that teaching children required a new, less adult-centered, more experience-based approach. Instead of having children sit at desks for hours every day memorizing and reciting teacher-dictated curriculum, John Dewey developed a progressive learning-by-doing approach to elementary education.

This Progressive approach allowed for the diverse needs, learning styles, and prior life experiences of the thousands of children of European immigrants who were pouring into the country to support the transition to an industrial economy. Dewey had observed that American educators were at a loss to reach these children academically, as well as socially and emotionally, pointing out that that their struggle to adjust to the many changes in their lives was causing social and behavioral issues at school (Flaherty & Osher, 2002).

John Dewey thought that the most effective educational approach for all children was one that engaged the whole child, kept children active, and gave them a hands-on way to learn about the culture, social interaction, and neighborhoods where they lived, while providing a deeper conceptual basis for reading, writing, and math.

During the era of Progressive education, for the first time, meeting the needs of public schoolchildren involved changing *how* schools approached learning, instead of punishing or excluding children who did not meet the expectations of educators. Dewey's writing highlighted the connection between public education and the nurturing of a democratic society. He encouraged active participation as a component of democratic process in schools, so that children would experience democracy at a young age and internalize its value.

Progressive education was born during the Progressive Era, when well-educated people and people of means considered investment in the well-being of impoverished immigrant families and their children as an investment in the future of the country. Settlement houses that offered an array of services to struggling families arose in cities, most often initiated and funded by women of means. These settlement houses also collaborated with schools to bring doctors and dentists into public schools for the first time, in order to attend to children whose health needs were not being met. The settlement houses developed collaborations with public schools to offer "vacation school" during the summertime, offering children activities and adult supervision while their parents were working (Flaherty & Osher, 2002).

The Progressive Era, including the years between 1899 and 1930, saw a widening circle of midwestern school communities that thrived using Dewey's model. In order to meet the needs of those children and families who were struggling, these Progressive schools engaged staff or collaborated with settlement houses to provide struggling children with "visiting teachers." Visiting teachers were the initial school social work-ers, making home visits to interact with and support families (Flaherty & Osher, 2002).

Volunteers and professionals often envisioned themselves as model citizens who were showing immigrants the way to become American. Although the services themselves were widely used and became a lifeline for many recipients, not all immigrant groups were eager to embrace the version of American identity that was being modeled by wealthy people who were culturally dissimilar. Progressive education itself also encoun-tered pockets of parental resistance to this active and unfamiliar version of school life, which did not rely entirely on traditional academic form and content.

This initial Progressive Era of public education collapsed with the Great Depression, as school budgets dried up and schools adopted a bare-bones, back-to-basics attitude. However, the Progressive model was preserved and further developed by institutions of higher learning such as Bennington College, Bank Street College of Education, and The Erickson Institute, and integrated into Canadian lab school practice by John Miller (1943/2010) in the 1940s.

Progressive public schools in America would reappear in some ur-ban and suburban areas during the more socially conscious period of the mid to late 1960s and early 1970s, running parallel to President Lyndon Johnson's Great Society initiative. Johnson's War on Poverty included Project Head Start, a preschool program for children whose families lived below the poverty line. In Project Head Start, active early learning and mental health support for preschool children and social support for their families were considered integral. For the first time, Project Head Start brought large numbers of young children of color into developmen-tally informed public early childhood education that incorporated the Progressive educational philosophy of learning by doing as well as parent participation and family support. Overwhelmingly positive outcomes from longitudinal study of high-quality, low-ratio early childhood programs for children in poverty included benefits such as increased high school gradua-tion rates, decreased teen pregnancy, lower rates of incarceration, and high employment and job satisfaction as young adults. A recent study of the Perry Preschool graduates, now in their 50s, found lasting benefits trans-ferred to their own children and grandchildren (Heckman & Karapakula, 2019; Schweinhardt, Barnes, & Weikart, 1993; Weikart, 1987). In ad-dition, Johnson's War on Poverty initiative included the passing of the Elementary and Secondary Schools Act of 1965, intended to promote quality and equity in public education. Funds were allocated for public schools in impoverished areas, to be used to offer a variety of services that addressed barriers to development and learning, including school-based health and mental health support, and expanding the number of school social workers in public schools. This allocation, known as Title I, is still in place today although less supportive of innovation and more stringently tied to supporting measures that improve test-score outcomes than was the case in the years prior to the Reagan administration.

Although Project Head Start and Title I have survived over the years, as have a small number of Progressive public elementary schools in New York, Boston, and other urban areas, political upheaval and the economic recession in the mid-1970s once again erased the "nonessential" educational components of social and emotional support as well as active learning in the majority of urban public schools.

During the financially stressed 1970s, the number of school social workers also diminished, and over time the role of social workers in schools shifted from the early emphasis on home visiting, to a focus on casework, to attendance-focused work, to a medical model of mental health support, to school adjustment and group work, and most recently to behavioral support in crisis situations. The majority of public school social work caseloads have become increasingly unwieldy, often requiring social workers to travel between several schools, or averaging 500 students per worker for those who provide services in one school. Therefore, the work has become crisis focused as less person power has been made available for the preventive, whole-child and whole-family interventions that once prevailed.

American Schools: Victims of the Cold War

Over the approximately 100-year evolution of public education in the United States, there has always been an interactive shifting tension between (and within) professionally informed educational practice, labor interests, and the politically driven federal educational agenda. The motivation to maintain a balance of these interest groups evaporated in 1983, when the Reagan administration released a report titled *A Nation at Risk* (National Commission on Excellence in Education, 1983), which condemned the quality of public education as part of his Cold War agenda to heighten competition with the Soviet Union.

Despite the fact that the educational outcomes data collected by the National Education Association (NEA) in the early 1980s actually showed increases in universal attendance, graduation rates, grades, and test scores, the highly publicized *A Nation at Risk* report told parents that their children's schools were abysmal and would lead to their children's incompetence as adults and their country's downfall (Mondale & Patton, 2001; Ravitch, 2020). This was the beginning of the politically driven "War on Public Education," where the impact of societal factors on learning was ignored, and high-stakes testing became the only measure of a school's success. Rather than acknowledge the effect of federally neglected social issues, politicians began to paint educators as unmotivated and incompetent.

Educational "reforms" based on the commission's study of the nation's public high schools were mandated for elementary schools and middle schools *as well as* high school, without regard to the needs and cognitive abilities of children at younger ages and stages. Although the knowledge base about child development and teaching and learning was already substantial, there was no effort to garner that knowledge to promote a stronger approach to teaching and learning in those states that were low on the NEA outcome measures. Although there was already a robust body of research connecting socioeconomic status with low performance in school, there were no new initiatives put into place to address the needs of families in poverty and no new supports provided for their children's schools.

This was the beginning of a politically driven corporate style "take over" of public education. It began with Reagan's encouragement of a business model for educational "reform," followed by George W. Bush's No Child Left Behind bill, mandating constant standardized testing as a requirement for schools receiving federal funds; to the Common Core curriculum that emerged during the Obama era; and perhaps now crescendoing with the Trump administration's appointment of Betsy DeVos as a secretary of education, whose overt agenda is not to support public education but to destroy it. The use of public funds to support privately run, for-profit charter schools serving primarily children of color that are encouraged by the Trump administration are considered unacceptable by the NAACP, citing frequent suspension, exclusion, military-style discipline, and cruelty to children as prevalent practice in these schools, while academic outcomes have been mixed (NAACP, 2016).

Teaching as a Political Act

Teaching and learning in the age of Trump goes beyond the 30-plus-year struggle of a profession kidnapped by politicians and their corporate sponsors. Schoolchildren of color whose parents watch the news, listen to radio, purchase newspapers, or give them access to the Internet take in overtly racist messages about people who look like them. They watch coverage of relatives, friends, or neighbors being handcuffed and loaded into Immigration and Customs Enforcement (ICE) vans. They watch elected officials work hard to undermine hard-won voting rights established as law decades ago. They listen to accounts of dangerous and illegal activities of people in power who remain in power, while their relatives sit in jail for minor offenses unable to make bail.

Children are learning in social studies textbooks that they are living in a democracy, but are experiencing a social order that doesn't resemble what they are reading about. When those in power deny children's experiential reality or mirror them and their families in a negative light, these messages distort self-image and undermine children's development, mental health, and motivation for mastery.

Teachers and school leaders themselves may struggle to make sense of what is happening in the world around them, let alone interpret those events to the children who depend on their guidance every day. The privacy of teachers and school leaders' own political identities, once seen as a private matter, now creates a challenge. Professionals who see the effects of regressive social policy in the eyes and anxious expressions of the faces that look up at them every morning become professionally responsible to acknowledge what they are seeing and hearing. Teachers, school leaders, and school social workers are in a position to acknowledge children's actual experiences and to reflect marginalized children in a positive light.

Teaching is a political act, whether or not that act is part of the school leader or teacher's identity, or a factor in their motivation to spend their days with children. Public schools are, by definition, an expression of the societal values and the political will and priorities that exist during a given period of time.

Although these values are subject to change, children's need for a meaningful and relevant education that nurtures their minds and hearts is a constant. When societal messages are antithetical to the well-being of schoolchildren, schools can work to counter these destructive messages, or will in essence promote them.

Access to supportive relationships at school is critical to all children's well-being no matter their economic status, race, cultural background, or birthplace. Ensuring that our children have access to a nurturing and meaningful education that supports emotional and social well-being in concert with intellectual growth is essential for everyone who wants to promote a safe and mentally healthy democratic society.

The continuing political impact of *A Nation at Risk* makes fighting for children's right to learn in developmentally meaningful ways, and acknowledging children's life experiences, an advocacy issue for teachers, school leaders, and parents.

SUPPORTING SOCIAL AND EMOTIONAL DEVELOPMENT IN SCHOOL

Although public school practice by and large remains score-driven and traditional in the United States in the first quarter of the 21st century, the groundswell of evidence pointing to the importance of supporting social and emotional development in schoolchildren has not been ignored. The high-profile incidents of destructive bullying and youth violence across the country, and the compelling outcomes of brain research and trauma-focused studies, have resulted in certain district mandates to implement some version of curriculum addressing social relationships, character education, emotional growth, or bullying prevention in public schools throughout our country.

Adding Social Emotional Learning: Does 1+1=2?

Social–Emotional Learning (SEL) programs can be useful and important additions to school life, helping schools to safeguard the social well-being of children as they move through the grades. However, instituting school-wide testing practices that *heighten* anxiety, pressure, and self-doubt in teachers, children, and parents, and *then* putting a social curriculum in place to help children cope with the anxiety *caused* by those measures is of questionable value. Adding "good practice after bad" may not sufficiently address the "common core" of children's social and emotional need to feel safe, accepted, competent, and seen in a positive light as an important member of their school communities.

When SEL programs are considered add-ons to a test-score-driven school culture, they are unlikely to succeed. In order to be effective, an SEL curriculum must be well integrated into the overall mission and climate of each school that implements it. It must be woven into the fabric of overall school practice. SEL programs that consist of discreet, time-limited curriculum or scripted interactions that run *parallel* to rigid school policies tend to focus less on promoting social and emotional *development* in children than on containing the expression of children's negative emotions in the school environment (Stearns, 2019). For example, a social curriculum that encourages children to increase their tolerance for peers who are different than they are has a lesser chance to be successful if the school itself has zero tolerance for children who learn or behave differently than their more focused peers.

Children who express feelings of powerlessness, vulnerability, or threat of inadequacy by becoming aggressive, disruptive, or distracting may not feel well supported by the school's social curriculum. In high pressure, test-score-driven schools, these behaviors are often seen as interfering with the mission of making sure that the other children are never distracted from their academic focus. This tension may be especially high in low-performing, high-poverty index schools, whose children are often highly stressed, and whose existence from one year to the next may depend on test score improvement. A child who acts out as a way of expressing emotional distress becomes a potential threat to the evaluation metrics of teachers and peers.

Typically, children who act out in school either come to school with issues that make them vulnerable, and/or develop feelings of vulnerability in response to an inappropriate educational environment. When the stakes are too high to invest in supporting vulnerable children through relationship-based practice, the SEL program may not offer a big-enough life raft for children who are treading water.

The Power of Teacher–Child Relationships

Emotionally Responsive Practice supports the contention that effective SEL programs depend on the cornerstone of supportive teacher–child relationships. There is compelling research that affirms the power of strong and supportive teacher–child relationships to foster both learning and social and emotional health. Hatfield and Williford (2016) found that close relationships between Head Start teachers and the children in their classrooms had long-lasting positive effects on behavior and academic success, as well as facilitating a drop in cortisol levels (stress hormone) compared to classrooms with less warmth. A recent multistate study on the role of close teacher–child relationships in kindergarten found teacher–child closeness predicted multiple positive academic and behavioral outcomes in children (Zulfiqar et al., 2018). Two other recent studies have found that positive and close teacher–child relationships can lessen depression in elementary school-children, as well as buffering vulnerable children from peer victimization (Elledge et al., 2016; Spilt et al., 2019).

A mega-analysis of the effect of teacher–child relationship quality on student engagement and achievement found positive associations between supportive relationships on both engagement and achievement, while negative relationships were associated with lower engagement and lower achievement. It is noted that negative relationships and low achievement intensify each other, leading to deeper issues over time (Rooda et al., 2011). In addition, the researchers were surprised by outcomes indicating that positive teacher–student relationships were important not only in early grades, but *remained* important across the school years, and had even *more* influence as a mediating factor for older low-performing children and low-SES children.

The Center on the Developing Child at Harvard University has made brain research available to educators, clinicians, and policymakers since 2000, producing a wealth of information relevant to public school practice. One of their early papers clearly outlines the connection between supportive early relationships and the development of brain architecture (National Scientific Council on the Developing Child, 2005). Another paper makes the connection between persistent fear and anxiety in childhood and impaired learning, explaining that the physiology of the brain is such that when stress hormones flood the hippocampus, higher-level cognition is impossible to access. When the hormonal flooding is chronic, neural connections that promote reasoning may be compromised (National Scientific Council on the Developing Child, 2010b). Subsequent research emphasizes the power of adult–child relationships to buffer toxic levels of stress and therefore allow children to have access to their own cognitive capacities (Darling-Hammond et al., 2020; National Scientific Council on the Developing Child, 2010a, 2010b, 2012, 2015, 2018).

Many well-known Americans who grew up in challenging circumstances credit their success to a teacher who saw their potential and helped them to see themselves in a positive light. These include Lyndon Johnson, Bill Clinton, Oprah Winfrey, Maya Angelou, Antwone Fisher, and Sonia Sotomayor to name a few. However, teachers who have been in the field for decades report less and less opportunity to interact with children and to get to know them well, as the demands of constant high-stakes assessment take their attention away from children's own agendas and increase teacher stress levels. In addition, veteran teachers and principals report a rise in both child and parent anxiety, creating a heightened need for support (Agna, G., & Black, B., personal communication, February 21, 2020).

There are many strategies that can be implemented to enhance potential for positive teacher–child relationships in public school. One such strategy is limiting class size. Several researchers have found that small class size consistently improves outcomes for young learners (Achilles

& Dun Schiffman, 2012; Dynarski et al., 2011; Heilig et al., 2010; Konstantopoulos & Chun, 2009). Although strong and positive teacher–child relationships with frequent interaction have been found to buffer levels of toxic stress in the lives of schoolchildren, small class size has not been championed by educational policymakers who are often driven by test scores, since the small class size approach is more costly.

Paradoxically, while politicians in the late 20th century and the early 21st century have increased the call for evidence-based practices to address unmet needs in education, there seems to be systemic denial of the mountains of evidence available to educators, child mental health specialists, and social policymakers concerning the efficacy of relationship-based practice to foster the social, emotional, and brain development that underlies learning in childhood, and to buffer the effects of the toxic stress and trauma.

Studies consistently point to poverty as the single most undermining factor for children's developmental outcomes. The Center for the Developing Child at Harvard have connected poverty-related conditions to enhanced vulnerability in the brain development of very young children (Jensen et al., 2017; Shonkoff, 2019). Poverty has also been found to result in an enhanced burden of anxiety and depression in school-aged children (Capistrano et al., 2016). In addition, poverty frequently diminishes access to resources that can provide protective factors for child health and mental health.

These findings dovetail with Stanford's recent comprehensive study of 8 years' worth of nationwide data concerning race, poverty, and school achievement. This research found that the school poverty rate is the most powerful factor to adversely impact school achievement, and to feed the achievement gap. The achievement gap, most often attributed to race, was found to be directly connected to concentration of poverty within school community. Since black and Hispanic families are more likely to reside in poor neighborhoods, the authors conclude that the achievement gap was erroneously contributed to race, rather than the core issue of community poverty (Reardon et al., 2020). However, educational pundits neglect to mention addressing poverty issues in their educational rhetoric, and antipoverty programs are absent from the federal agenda in the age of Trump.

When the federal discourse reflects vulnerable groups of children and adults in a negative light, it distorts their reality, creating confusion, doubt, fear, and feelings of inadequacy in both children and the parents and teachers who care for them. This negative portrayal becomes a "bad mirror," meaning, an inaccurate reflection of who they are, endangering self-worth and motivation in large numbers of our public school children and their teachers.

Teachers and school leaders may find themselves identifying with the experience of being distorted by facing so many "broken mirrors." They work hard to give children a strong foundation, but do so with the knowledge that the powers that be don't consider them or the children that they teach worthy of investment in professionally recommended strategies for success. They live with the knowledge that in 2020, their children's needs are regarded as "inconvenient truths" by those who have the power to address them. The message is that the known remedies are too costly to implement. In reality, the cost of ignoring those remedies is much, much higher.

The Emperor Has No Clothes!

In the children's tale, *The Emperor's New Clothes*, a vain emperor was tricked into believing that he was wearing fine clothes made of cloth so special that only intelligent people could appreciate them. He himself could see no clothes on his body, but he feared were he to acknowledge that, his subjects would think him stupid. He paraded into the town square with nothing on to show the townspeople his "special new clothes." Only an innocent child among the crowd of townspeople pointed out that the emperor was indeed wearing nothing.

In the tale of *The Wizard of Oz*, a so-called wizard ruled the Land of Oz by disguising himself as an all-knowing, omnipotent, and terrifying creature. A little girl and her dog finally exposed the ordinary human hiding behind the curtain who projected the illusion of the scary creature and controlled the sound and visual effects that kept the citizens at bay.

Unfortunately, in the real-life story of our public schools, children are not in the position to reveal the truth about how high-pressure "reforms" affect their day-to-day lives in school, nor point out that those in charge of creating educational mandates are not experts in child development or learning. Neither are children able to articulate the damage being done to their self-image, racial, and cultural identity and sense of belonging when powerful people demean them and seek to incarcerate or deport people who look like them.

The promise of public school in our times is to acknowledge and harness the power of parents, teachers, school leaders, and school mental health staff to become "good mirrors" for the children in their care and good advocates for feeding their social, emotional, and intellectual potential. The tools of Emotionally Responsive Practice may help the local heroes who work in public education do their best work as well as to advocate for promising practices within school community. Until we can "expose the man behind the curtain," it is crucial for people who care about children to stay connected to the true stories of our collective experience in public school.

CHAPTER 2

Looking Through the Lens of Development

Children develop within the context of relationship. When children are small, their relationship circles are also small. There may be parents and grandparents. There may be aunts and uncles. There may be a neighbor or caregiver. Within these small circles, a young child is held. Within these small circles, the child's development unfolds. The debate about whether it is nature or nurture that determines developmental outcomes has become obsolete, with brain research showing us that a child's innate capacities are in part *experience dependent* in order to blossom in joyful ways. Responsive, nurturing care, and loving communication between adults and their young children feed the developing brain. Reciprocal interactions with adult caregivers stimulate and carve neural pathways and promote integral connections within the brain, creating an infrastructure for reading the world socially, emotionally, and cognitively (National Scientific Counsel on the Developing Child, 2018). Therefore, developmental outcomes are partially determined by the young child's access to at least one available and loving adult partner. To accomplish essential developmental milestones, infants, toddlers, and young children may need all the adults who spend many hours a day with them to become engaged in developmental partnership.

SUPPORTING DEVELOPMENTAL FOUNDATIONS FOR GROUP LIFE

Children enter group child-care or classroom life at various ages in different parts of our country. Some families have the resources and desire to obtain high-quality infant and toddler group care. Others need the care but do not have the resources to obtain it. Many children enter early childhood programs at 3 or 4 years of age, as both public and private options begin to expand in most states. Still other children enter the school setting at age 5 or 6. With the possible exception of home-schooled children, the majority of American children experience group life in their early years. This means that an early childhood or elementary school program has the potential to be "the biggest umbrella" for sheltering vulnerable children, and protecting their right to develop social, emotional, and cognitive learning within supportive teacher–child relationships. No matter where children are along the developmental continuum, they will need adult partnerships during the several hours each day that they spend in educational settings.

To thrive in group life, young children need to feel comfortable and safe when surrounded by other children. They need to feel free to explore the early childhood environment, and to use the materials available to them in developmentally salient ways. Most important, they need to have strong relationships with the adults who are caring for them. They need those adults to have an agenda that mirrors their own, so that they can use the early care environment to discover themselves and discover others without being disrupted or derailed by an external agenda. A toddler who is busy connecting giant popping beads and then pulling them apart cannot focus on his developmental mission of exploring "together and apart" if a teacher keeps prompting him to count the beads instead, so that she can check this prescribed skill off of her list. A young child who is sobbing as she separates from her grandmother cannot focus on connecting her sad feelings with the departure of her primary caregiver when her teacher is asking her to "smile so her face will look pretty."

A look through the lens of development gives teachers and caregivers a window into the meaning behind children's behavior and play. This view allows teachers and caregivers to join the children in their developmental process of growing and learning. This is true for teachers of 2-year-olds as well as teachers of 10-year-olds. Moving away from external standards that program teachers to focus on what children *should be* doing instead of looking into the developmental meaning of what children are *actually* motivated to do can free teachers from the treadmill of pressuring children to perform in ways that may lack meaning. An external, standards-driven focus can pull teachers' attention away from the children in front of them at an age where development demands connection. Looking through the lens of development allows teachers and caregivers to find and connect with children of all ages *where they are*, in order to partner with them and support the resolution of the foundational developmental milestones that allow for more sophisticated levels of mastery as children grow.

THE AGE OF OPPORTUNITY

When children enter kindergarten, they are assumed to be old enough to have mastered saying good-bye and separating from family, engaging with other children, and using their teacher as a resource when feeling confused or needing comfort. These days 5-year-olds are also assumed to be ready to master reading and writing, remain seated for most of the day, and tolerate the several transitions that every school day includes.

These assumptions paint a picture of prior opportunity for the vast majority of very young children in our country. In this picture, babies, toddlers, and preschool children have *already* had enough time in the care of attached, nurturing adults. They have *already* had enough time and safe spaces to develop the capacity for symbolic, creative play. They have *already* had consistent caregiving relationships in safe environments that allowed for exploration and hands-on learning. Therefore, they *should* be ready to meet academic expectations! The problem with that picture is that it does not reflect reality for large numbers of children. Sadly, for many children, the school setting may be their *first* real opportunity to feel safe and cared for, since unmet survival needs may intrude on parents' ability to be present for their children. For many children, the age of opportunity is the age that they reach when finally entering a school or caregiving community that will allow them to gather the relationship support needed to resolve the early milestones that will enhance stability and empower lifelong learning.

FIRST THINGS FIRST: ESSENTIAL MILESTONES
FOR HEALTHY DEVELOPMENT

Since the developmental process is in part experience-dependent, and since research finds that thousands of American families struggle to meet their children's basic needs due to reasons that include poverty, trauma, and addiction, it is reasonable to conclude that many children enter school without having had opportunities for supportive developmental partnerships. Of course, since infants, toddlers, and preschool children in early childhood programs are *still in the process* of working out early developmental issues, they need developmental partners 24 hours a day, including the hours that they spend in child care and school. Healing early education environments understand the importance of their facilitative role in children's developmental process, and organize around supporting the foundational social and emotional milestones shown in Figure 2.1.

Figure 2.1. Developmental Milestones for Social Emotional Growth

0–1	1–2	2–3	3–4	4–5
Reciprocity, Nurture, Attunement ⇩ Attachment ⇩ Regulation of State ⇩ Symbiosis ⇩ Differentiation ⇩ Object Permanence ⇩ Pointing and Labeling	Locomotion ⇩ Psychological Home Base ⇩ Transitional Object ⇩ Language Bridge ⇩ Early Level Symbolic Play ⇩ Separation Issues in Behavior and Play Ambivalence	Autonomy ⇩ "No" and "Mine" ⇩ Toileting ⇩ Body Integrity Issues ⇩ Integration of Positive and Negative Affects ⇩ Object Constancy ⇩ Symbolic Play Sequences Elaborate	Mastery ⇩ "Why" ⇩ Cause and Effect Relationship ⇩ Parallel Play ⇩ Cooperative Play, Dramatic ⇩ Same and Different ⇩ Monsters, Dreams	Peer Group ⇩ "Are You My Friend?" ⇩ Identity Issues ⇩ Gender ⇩ Power vs. Powerlessness ⇩ Body Integrity ⇩ Birth, Death, Injury ⇩ Fantasy vs. Reality

5–6	6–7	7–8	8–9
Need to compete and win; feels powerless easily ⇩ Identity issues dominate ⇩ Gender is a more salient identity maker ⇩ Authority issues are evident ⇩ License with truth is common ⇩ Royalty and dinosaurs are play themes	Same sex friendships dominate ⇩ Peer group pull increases ⇩ Concern about self presentation increases ⇩ Roles of inventor, builder, and detective are satisfying ⇩ Fantasy and reality factors are both used to explain perceptions and inform play ⇩ Interests and talents emerge ⇩ New level of individuation from parents is evident	Conceptual intelligence is evident ⇩ Fantasy and reality lines are more clearly drawn ⇩ "Best Friend" or group member is important ⇩ Group projects are motivating and satisfying ⇩ Inadequacy stimulated by peer rejection or not achieving in school	Needs to perceive meaning in academic material in order to thrive in class ⇩ Internalizes feelings of inadequacy or acts them out ⇩ Can argue position coherently ⇩ Can look at past, present, and future on new level ⇩ Image of self includes dreams and fears of future

Although many school-based professionals studied child development in college, the immediacy of classroom life, administrative demands, and the range of chronological ages of the children being taught may make the study of child development seem like a distant memory. Working teachers may consider their prior learning as academic theory that doesn't readily apply to classroom practice. They may set it aside like an old book to gather dust on a shelf. However, Emotionally Responsive Practice (ERP) classrooms differ in an important way. In ERP-identified schools, teachers use their knowledge of child development to inform classroom practice every single day.

Although all of the developmental milestones shown in Figure 2.1 are salient precursors for children's comfort with group life, connection to self and others, and curious, attentive, receptive learning, those milestones explored in more detail in the sections below have profound implications for children's classroom functioning. Unresolved, these milestones will make school life challenging for children at every age.

Attachment

Attachment is the cornerstone of social and emotional development. Since children's brains, bodies, and hearts develop within the context of attachment relationships, attachment is an essential ingredient in a child's developmental process. If children cannot attach, or if there are no consistent adults to attach to, developmental process is compromised. Babies and toddlers spend hours every day studying their attachment partners' faces and affects. If babies see a loving expression, they respond with contentment. If babies see a distressed or distracted affect, they respond with emotional disequilibrium (Beebe & Steele, 2013). Babies learn about self and other within attachment relationships. They learn about reciprocal communication when their parents interact playfully in response to their coos and babbles. They learn about connection and empathy when their attached adults mirror their distressed expressions and sounds with an empathic tone and expression, communicating that the attachment relationship can appreciate and hold the baby through all kinds of feelings.

Attachment can be thought about on an experiential continuum. When children have no opportunity to attach, because interaction with adults is extremely minimal and basic needs for holding and feeding go unattended (as may be the case in extremely underfunded orphanage care), children's brains actually shrink due to neglect (National Scientific Counsel on the Developing Child, 2012).

When children have the opportunity to attach, but their attachment partners are inconsistent, disengaged, erratic, or emotionally unavailable due to physical or mental illness, domestic violence, substance abuse, or other extremely stressful circumstances, the attachment may become anxious or insecure. An anxiously attached child is never sure what the attachment relationship has to offer from one moment or one day to the next. It becomes difficult for anxiously attached children to feel secure within this relationship (Ainsworth et al., 1987). It also becomes impossible for young children to organize themselves around these relationships, because they are unpredictable. Since attachment relationships are the base from which the child explores the world, the exploration process may be more difficult in the absence of a secure attachment.

Attachment has different functions at different ages and stages throughout the life cycle. In infancy, attachment relationships provide a soothing context for babies to move from one physical and emotional state to another. For example, it is the attachment figure whose response allows the baby to move from a state of hunger to a state of being full and satisfied. It is the attachment figure whose voice in song weaves a path for an overly stimulated and screaming baby to become a sleeping and content baby. In toddlerhood, it is the attachment partner who encourages the standing, cruising toddler to become a walking toddler by welcoming the transition with open arms. In order for early transitions to be resolve well, children need their attachment partners to pave the way.

In infancy, baby and parent can experience a period of existing with one another within an "attachment bubble" that does not allow the rest of the world to enter. Margaret Mahler referred to this feeling of oneness as *symbiosis* (Mahler et al., 1985/2018). This early time of life within a bubble has protective value for the infant. Although parent and baby may be walking on a crowded, noisy street with blaring sirens and honking horns, the baby in the parent's snuggly hears the rhythm of the parent's heartbeat; feels the rhythm of her walk, the warmth of her body, and the vibration of her reassuring voice; and is locked in moments of mutual eye gaze. Essentially, the intimacy of this early attachment phase protects the baby from the intrusion of an overstimulating big world. In Mahler's language, the infant "hatches out" of this bubble at approximately 4 months, as grabbing and exploring the physical world becomes physically possible and compelling (Mahler et al., 1985/2018).

For parent–child attachment partnerships to work well, the adult needs to keep up with the baby's gradual but never-ending developmental pull for separation and individuation. In other words, as children grow, what children need from attachment partners changes. Parenting missions move from nurturing, to limit setting, to interpreting the world of family and friends and beyond (Galinsky, 1987). When parents do not make these developmental transitions alongside their children, children may struggle to make them alone.

Tragically, attached children sometimes experience early loss of their primary caregivers and attachment partners due to sudden changes in family structure, migration and deportation, incarceration, illness, or death. Disruptions in attachment relationships can disrupt the developmental process, as the adversity of loss may overwhelm a child's capacity to cope with age-appropriate challenges.

Because development happens in the context of loving relationships, initial attachment relationships impact children's receptivity to the attachment relationships that follow. One of the most powerful adult–child relationships outside of home for most children is the relationship with their teacher.

At School. Well-attached children who have had consistent and loving experiences with adults in early life typically come to school expecting their teachers and caregivers to be caring and responsive. Although a young child may initially be hesitant to engage an unfamiliar adult in an unfamiliar classroom, over time, a securely attached child is likely to be open to engaging in a trusting relationship with a responsive teacher. Secure and undisrupted attachment relationships in early life set the stage for receptivity to other healthy relationships as children grow.

When a teacher is not available as an attachment partner, because building nurturing relationships with children is not a priority, children who have strong attachment partnerships at home may feel lonely in the classroom, but can most often stay connected to their peers and to the curriculum given the absence of learning disabilities or trauma.

Children who have not had prior opportunity to become attached to a nurturing adult, who have insecure attachments, who have had primary attachment relationships disrupted by loss or abrupt separation, or who have developmental differences or traumatic history, most often cannot thrive in the classroom without the availability of the teacher as developmental partner. When the everyday experience of school life does not include an available attachment partner, children with attachment needs are often at a loss. They may act out, seek attention but avoid connection, underperform, be disorganized, relate indiscriminately, or seem oblivious to the teacher's wishes or directions. Since attachment is a developmental cornerstone, the older children get without opportunities for strong attachments to adults, the more essential developmental missions may go unresolved. This may be true for children growing up in poverty within the foster care system, as well as children of the 1% who may rarely see their parents and have a revolving series of nannies caring for them.

Fortunately, positive teacher–child relationships can be very powerful to a young child. Research finds that warm relationships with children's first teachers predict social, emotional, and cognitive strength throughout the school years (Hatfield & Williford, 2016; Zulfiqar et al., 2018). The impact of strong and nurturing teacher–child relationships is found to be the most powerful for children who perform poorly, and children who come to school with heightened social and emotional vulnerability (Roorda et al., 2011). Given these findings, and given that there are always children present in classrooms who need relationship support, opportunity for teacher–child attachment becomes an essential element of ERP.

Differentiation and Object Permanence

As babies become toddlers and toddlers become preschool children, little by little they begin to differentiate themselves from things and people in their intimate environments. This process of differentiation continues cognitively, socially, and emotionally as children grow. For example, babies who grab and mouth objects at 4 or 5 months might subsequently drop an item that moments before was satisfying to explore. When this happens, they don't pursue the object, express distress, or try to reach for it. For infants, a dropped object out of their sensory field is "all gone." Things only exist as the taste, smell, sight, or sound that they provide upon interaction. When providing sensory input, an item becomes part of the sensory self. Without sensory-based interaction, the item no longer exists for the baby. Even at 6 months, a baby who is crawling toward a coveted toy stops crawling when the toy is covered by a blanket as the infant approaches. Once covered, there is no sensory connection, and the toy is "all gone."

Babies and young toddlers brilliantly engage their attachment partners in playful interactions that help build developmental bridges to more differentiated relationships within the intimate environment. The 8-month-old may stand up in her crib, look at her attachment partner, and take the toy from her mouth and send it tumbling out of the crib, onto the floor. A responsive caregiver picks it up and hands it back, causing a joyful reunion for the baby, who, moments later, does the same thing again! This repetitive game of "toy peek-a-boo" lends an experiential foundation for the soon-to-develop capacity for object permanence.

Between 9 and 12 months, well-attached, well-supported children who have not experienced major disruption typically begin to seek, react to, or act to recover dropped objects. Development and experience come together to support the attainment of object permanence. The baby now knows that objects exist apart from self. They exist even when out of sight, earshot, or reach. Therefore, things in the environment inspire even more curiosity and deeper levels of exploration. Well-attached children begin to point to objects and look to their attachment figures to provide meaningful labels. Often, this process of codefining the world with parents and caregivers heralds the baby's first words, as babies begin to repeat the labels given to them. First words are an occasion for rejoicing, as families watch a baby's language come to life within loving relationships (Stearns & Stearns, 1985).

At School. There are many routines and expectations integrated into early childhood programs that assume object permanence is in place in order for children to fully engage. There are many transitions involved in group life that require children to have attained a solid sense of object permanence is order to go smoothly. Since very young toddlers may not have reached this important milestone, as well as other markers of differentiation, and since older toddlers may still be in process, it is necessary to keep ratios low in infant–toddler care. Adults need to be available to support children's interactions and explorations as well as to shepherd them through every transition. When toddlers become preschool children and eventually elementary school children, teacher-to-child ratios can be increased. Classroom life is often organized around encouraging children to function independently. Independent functioning looks quite different when children's early experiences have supported the developmental process.

For example, Dante, who is securely attached and able to separate from the adult who brings him to school, is also independent in his choice of play materials. He is pretending to be a firefighter, using props that he has differentiated from self and able to use to represent others. Dante often tells the teachers that he will be a firefighter when he is big. When it is clean-up time, Dante's knowledge of object permanence allows him to put the props away, secure in the knowledge that they will still be there the next time he needs them, even though out of sight and touch for now.

Dante's cubby partner Craig has had many disruptions in his 3 and a half years of life. He zooms into the classroom and grabs every interesting thing in sight, ending up holding on to a large collection of random items that make constructive interaction difficult. He does not differentiate the way he plays with one toy verses the other. When clean-up time comes, Craig cannot clean up independently. The teacher gently guides him toward letting go of the materials that he has collected so that he can put them away. Craig screams, throws his toys, hits and sobs, having no faith that those toys will ever be retrievable, once out of sensory contact.

The children's stressed teacher notes that almost all transitions seem impossible for Craig, but feels that her expectations are age-appropriate, and becomes frustrated when these scenarios play themselves out day after day, despite having given Craig extra notice about when clean-up time is coming. When the children rush into the room in the morning, and the teacher notices that Craig is absent that day, she breathes a sigh of relief. When Craig comes back the next day, he feels his teacher's ambivalence as she greets him.

Psychological Home Base

Securely attached young toddlers who are beginning to walk use their attachment partners as a home base. They may start out playing very close by their partner, but after a while, something interesting may compel a journey across the room in order to explore an interesting item. Very often toddlers pick up whatever has been discovered and walk gleefully back to their attachment partners to share their discoveries. Parent and child codiscover and codefine the item, the adult providing language and perhaps demonstrating its potential use. The satisfied toddler leaves her discovery in her parent's lap, and happily begins another journey. Soon, the adult has a lap full of the room, and the toddler has practiced mini-separations, autonomous discovery, and reunion. Going away from her attachment partner and coming back to her many times allows the toddler to move away little by little, without feeling disconnected or disoriented. The attached adult who partners with the toddler gives her an experiential foundation for using relationship as a safe base from which to go forth, as well as to anticipate receptive connection upon return.

At School. Well-developing children who have had experiential support for the attainment of psychological home base come to the childcare or school environment expecting to organize and orient themselves using relationships with responsive adults. When in doubt, they look to the adult. When they make discoveries, they proudly show the adult. When they need help, they come to the adult.

Children who have not had experiential support for the attainment of psychological home base may lack this orientation. In the classroom, they may seem to lack direction and initiative, or need permission in order to take action in any way. Conversely, children without psychological home base are often very active but extremely disorganized. Since they may not use the teachers as a point of orientation, they may seem to be everywhere and nowhere, moving constantly but not settling long enough to truly explore or engage. When in need of direction, they may follow another child's lead, instead of coming to the adult. These patterns can become problematic as expectations for organization and self-regulation increase with age.

Early Level Separation: Transitional Objects

Young toddlers may be content with their small journeys into the immediate environment, with the adult nearby. Older toddlers, who are more secure walkers and are beginning to jump and run, may be compelled to explore beyond what is in front of them. They may want to go pull everything out of the kitchen cupboard while their parents are on the phone in the bedroom. They may want to go upstairs when their caregiving grandparents are downstairs. In order to have the psychological freedom that allows them to feel emotionally safe and connected even when gaining more and more physical distance from attachment partners, older toddlers may invent transitional objects (TOs). TOs are objects from the intimate environment that come to represent the child's attachment relationship.

TOs are often stuffed animals, small soft blankets, and other comfort objects that become symbols of connection to attachment partners. Although, well-supported toddlers may develop object permanence between 9 and 12 months, they are not able to reliably conjure up the image of their attachment partners when out of sight until between 28 and 36 months. TOs that may smell like mama, be used by dada to cover them, or have been given to them by grandma become a way of holding on to family when physically separate. The existence of a TO in a child's life is a positive developmental indicator. It means that the child has at least one attachment partner, since the object is a symbol for that relationship. It also demonstrates the toddler's ability to create a symbol. Making one thing stand for another is a core and critical developmental capacity, underlying emergent symbolic play as a way to represent and integrate feeling and experience, as well as emergent literacy as children grow toward school age.

Some toddlers find other ways to solve the developmental dilemma of becoming physically separate before they achieve object constancy, which is the ability to bring the attachment figure to mind, even when apart. But transitional objects are useful for many toddlers as a developmental bridge to individuation. An 18-month-old can tolerate the separation that naptime brings with her "blankey" in hand. A 22-month-old can wave bye-bye and soon recover from a daily separation with his teddy bear held tightly.

At School. Toddlers, preschool children, and kindergarteners often bring their TOs to school. Teachers who understand the developmental significance of TOs know that the children who bring their TOs usually need them in order to make a positive adjustment to the school environment. Indeed, TOs can be used intentionally as part of classroom life and curriculum throughout the elementary grades to support teacher–child connection, encourage the use of symbol and metaphor, and promote prosocial interaction within the peer community (Koplow, 2008). However, if TOs are prohibited, children who still need them may be at a loss to self-comfort, make transitions, or feel safe enough to engage in curricular activities. The more vulnerable children feel at school, the more likely they are to use preemptive aggression to protect themselves, or to become victims of other children's aggression.

Rather than consider TO use a problem to be forbidden, Emotionally Responsive school communities integrate TOs into school life in order to strengthen the foundations of relationship, develop symbolic play and symbolic thought, and help children to feel secure at school.

Symbolic Social Narrative in Play

Children's first words usually reference experience shared with an attachment partner or simply serve to label the attachment partner (*mama*, *dada*, and so forth). A child points to something that both he and his parent can see and announces its name, which has been spoken by the parent so many times before. Later in toddlerhood when children begin to spontaneously put two words together, language begins to bridge ideas as well as to bridge separation. The toddler who gets her doll and then fetches a small blanket to cover her, looks up, and says, "baby sleep," putting one finger on her lip and whispering, "shhh." The toddler who has been drinking milk from a sippy cup but has dropped it, runs to his caregiver in the next room saying, "Uh-oh! Milky!"

These utterances serve important new functions as toddlers discover ways to code and symbolize the many new discoveries that standing and walking bring, and as they begin to develop language that allows them to share these experiences with others. A symbolic social narrative begins to develop that includes both language and play symbols as vehicles for connection on an emotional, social, and cognitive level. When children are interacting with adults who reflect the toddlers' narration of experience with interest and empathy, the birth of symbolic narrative in language and play expands day by day. When adults use language to affirm, elaborate, and respond to language and play symbols by joining toddlers in their developmental space, children learn that adult–child relationships are fertile ground for the birth of mutually meaningful symbolic constructs.

When very young children in a group setting are using toys to imitate life routines, like eating and sleeping, other children recognize those play scenarios as meaningful representations of their own experience as well and may join in. As children move from imitative play to symbolic play in older toddlerhood, play increasingly becomes a primary vehicle for representing and working out developmental and life experience issues. Play that is developmentally salient draws other children in like a magnet, increasingly giving children opportunities to cocreate with peers as they move into the early childhood years.

When young children are exploring materials and constructing meaningful play sequences, themes that reflect developmental issues and conflicts are almost always present. Play around separation and rejoining (together and apart, sleeping and waking), owning (packing, claiming, hoarding, having a lot), and emergent identity (dressing up, baby and caregiver, doggie and kitty, etc.) are pervasive themes in healthy representational play. The familiar themes support the development of social narrative as children discover that their symbolic portrayals are meaningful to others as well.

As children move into the preschool years, superheroes and other powerful characters emerge as part of the social narrative, giving children a common ground for connecting to and cocreating developmentally compelling narratives that allow them to represent and integrate issues of identity and power.

The development of early language and early representational play run parallel, and together these emerging capacities allow social play to be infused with communicative intent. As play narratives become increasingly rich, with both personal and social meaning, children create expressive pathways that deepen the connection of emergent self to a community of peers.

When children become exposed to media that provides its own themes and imagery, the peer narrative can become increasingly dominated by the mutual knowledge and connection to the characters and action presented in the virtual world. Constant exposure to age-inappropriate media imagery at very young ages can overwhelm and overstimulate children to the point that they are compelled to master the media content in play by repeating it, sometimes abandoning the self-generated play dialogues that evolve from inner life, symbolic development, and the mutual experiences that inform a rich social narrative. This form of media "addiction" can be confusing to parents, who may mistake children's preoccupation with media as a sign of interest, and respond by providing more and more opportunities for exposure.

At School. When children enter school without prior relationship support for the development of language that codefines their worlds and bridges, separation, there is frequently a lack of evolution in the development of play symbols as well as spoken vocabulary. Since play symbols serve as building blocks for social connection, and allow for developmental integration, they are indispensable tools in group life. Elementary school teachers who have consulted with the Center for Emotionally Responsive Practice at Bank Street College of Education have commented that in recent years, there has been an increase in children who come to school without these important foundational social play skills across the socioeconomic spectrum.

A number of societal changes may contribute to the differences in social narrative skills that teachers are observing. The decline in the quality of social language and play in both lower-income and higher-income groups may in large part be attributed to the impact of ever-present technology in the lives of children and their parents. The pervasive presence of screens in the day-to-day lives of children and parents has a ripple effect on developmental process. It often diminishes parental availability and encourages children to follow suit by becoming mesmerized by screen sound and imagery instead of engaging directly with parents, siblings, and other family members. In addition, the connection between increasing amounts of screen time and decreasing amounts of unstructured, outdoor play has been well documented as a public health concern (Sigman, 2019; Yogman et al., 2018).

Frequently, children who want parental attention while their parents are otherwise engaged are also referred to smart phones or tablets as a remedy. This pattern has been observed both in low-income and higher-income communities.

There have been many studies that focus on the vast differences in the lower rate of vocabulary acquisition for children living in poverty, relative to higher-income peers. One study of parent–toddler interaction in middle-income communities revealed a lessening of parent–child interaction/conversation in recent years, as children struggle to compete with their parents' involvement with ever-present devices. The result was a lessening of the vocabulary gap as middle- and upper-income children's vocabulary declined.

Although there has been a consistent focus on income-related gaps in vocabulary acquisition over time, there has been less emphasis on income-related differences in social narrative that includes *both* language development and the development of symbolic play. Poverty creates a vulnerability to highly stressful circumstances such as homelessness, hunger, neglect, domestic violence, and incarceration. These adverse experiences can simultaneously *diminish* opportunities for the relationship support that comes from well-protected parent–child reciprocal interactions, and *heighten* the child's need for the symbolic tools of social narrative that allow for emotional integration of difficult experience within community. Public school is the community that has the most potential to provide and enhance the capacity for symbolic processes for all of our children.

Teachers of young children know this, but report feeling more pressure than ever before to limit or exclude play in pre-K, kindergarten, and early grade classrooms for fear that they will not have enough time for standards-driven curriculum. Indeed, the pressure for elementary schools to give mountains of homework, related to anxieties about test-score outcomes, eats up school hours, as well as out-of-school hours, and becomes an additional stressor for exhausted children and their exhausted parents at the end of the day.

The imposition of structure in both children's in-school and out-of-school time has become a national norm at younger and younger ages. Although research has shown that enrolling young children in structured after-school skills-focused classes, such as ballet, chess, and similar activities, has no long-term value (Schiffrin et al., 2015), parents continue to opt for structured activities over open-ended downtime.

All of these factors create a perfect storm for an increase in social and emotional isolation and the resulting behavioral and mood disturbances that both communicate our children's pain and strain classroom dynamics. If children lack opportunity for open-ended, creative, constructive play in their lives outside of school, it is extremely important that opportunities to develop self-generated, inventive, social play be integrated into the school day. Given that symbolic play narratives facilitate social connection, symbolic and abstract thinking, self-regulation, and the integration of emotionally challenging experiences, children without protected time and space for open-ended social play are at a loss. As opportunities for unstructured play have declined, mental health problems in children, teens, and young adults have increased (Grey, 2010; Yogman et al., 2018).

Separation/Individuation ("No" and "Mine")

Since walking toddlers may be experiencing more and more time physically separate from attachment partners, they are called on to differentiate, or individuate, themselves from their partners (Mahler et al., 1985/2018). This is a process that happens throughout toddlerhood but often peeks between 18 and 28 months. Very young children seek to feel their separate selves by opposing the adults' wishes, and by taking ownership of everything that they encounter. Therefore, "no" and "mine!" become the individuating toddler's favorite words. This is an important time for the autonomy-seeking toddler, who needs to both oppose important adults and continue to be nurtured and sustained by them. Young children need their attachment relationships to be strong enough to hold their developmentally inspired negativity. This can be a challenging time for parents, who might not know where all of this negative energy is coming from!

During this period, children need to know that parents can see, hear, and empathize with their need to do the opposite and allow for the expression of negative affects, but will not abdicate authority. In other words, it is very hard to oppose a force that keeps coming over to your side of the fence! In order for toddlers' negativity to have developmental value, their adult partners in development need to have empathy for their toddlers' anger and distress, but keep setting reasonable limits so that children feel safe and protected, while supporting the individuation process. Although young children may scream and cry when their "no" is overridden, they feel a distinctive and individuating self in the process of emerging when their feeling states and wishes are not the same as those of their attachment partners.

This essential mission of individuation can become difficult to accomplish when circumstances do not support it. If there is no permission to express negativity within the parent–child relationship, developmental resolution isn't supported. If parents can't tolerate the anger and tantrums that might come as a result of limit setting and give toddlers free reign, there is nothing for them to oppose, and the mission of individuation is compromised.

At School. "No" and "mine" come to school whether a teacher is teaching 2-year-olds or 10-year-olds. When the individuation process is not resolved, children will try again. When the parent–child relationship cannot hold negativity, children may wait for a relationship with an adult that will support their developmental process. For many children, this adult is likely to be their teacher, who spends several hours a day in their company, and returns to the classroom day after day. A child in need of adult partnership for the individuation process may be relatively compliant during the first weeks of school, as she considers whether this new adult is safe and can withstand emotional storms. Once positively assessed, the negative voice may have a constant presence.

Because oppositional behavior is annoying and can feel very personal, teachers may react with impatience, and eventually with disdain. Children then experience their developmentally motivated negativity as "bad," which often results in an escalation of the oppositional behavior and power struggle, as they fight to defend a fragile self-image. There is a danger that children will get sucked into seeing themselves in the "bad mirror" that has come to reflect and define their relationships with adults, and then with other children in the school setting.

For children who have never spent time with an adult who set limits, the existence of classroom structures and predetermined routines can be a shock. Although being "in charge" at a young age is profoundly anxiety inducing for children, it is can be a rude awakening for these children when teachers naturally assume that they are the ones to determine the course of events in the classroom.

Although "no" and "mine" make the classroom dynamic complicated, understanding the underlying issues can be a relief to teachers and school leaders, who may be able to offer more school friendly opportunities for children to express a negative voice.

Integration of Positive and Negative Affects/Experiences

One of the paradoxes of child development is that while object permanence, the ability to differentiate self from items in the environment and to know that these items exist whether they are in sight or within reach or not, typically happens for well-supported children between 9 and 12 months of age, object constancy, the ability to carry the attachment partner internally when physically separate, takes much longer to achieve. For object constancy to be possible, the very young child needs the other foundational milestones discussed in this chapter to be in place. In addition, the toddler must integrate both passive and negative affects experienced within their intimate caregiving relationships.

All children have both positive and negative experiences with their attachment partners. The same parent who is generally nurturing might be exhausted and impatient at the end of the day. The same grandparent who is almost always responsive might not be feeling well and might neglect to respond. When adult–child interactions weigh on the side of the positive, over time children can accommodate the negative and internalize a stable, comforting parental image to take with them when physically separate.

When adult–child relationships weigh on the side of the negative, or there is too much polarity in the caregiving affects, this integration becomes problematic. A child whose parent offers a bottle of milk one minute, and injures him in a fit of rage the next minute, cannot integrate those two disparate experiences. Instead, the child most often keeps them separate, staying connected to the possibility of nurture but cutting himself off from the abusive elements and attributing the danger elsewhere. Although a child may not have a conscious connection to the abusive events, his physiology organizes itself around the chronic stress that the traumatic events caused, and often results in an uneasy hyperalertness to adult affects and actions.

This integration of positive and negative affects may also be disrupted by domestic violence. Although rage and violent behavior may not necessarily be directed at the young child, observing violent behavior between parents whom she loves and depends on is emotionally overwhelming, fear inducing, and a constant source of toxic stress.

When caregiving behavior and parental interaction are erratic and dangerous, young children may experience negative emotions in themselves and in others as potentially destructive, making them unable to integrate. When negative emotions are experienced as dangerous intrusions, the child's capacity to integrate them is overwhelmed, and the ability to develop social–emotional cause and effect can be inhibited. Sometimes, children in this situation are vulnerable to being taken over by negative outbursts without connecting to where their feelings are coming from. The ability to take next steps forward on the social–emotional developmental continuum may seem to be paralyzed.

At School. Children who come to school without having integrated both positive and negative experiences within relationships with primary adults are frequently difficult to read, wary of adults and other children, isolated, unpredictable, and explosive. We know that from infancy, babies are focused on parental affects as a way of understanding emotion and feeling connected and safe. Children who have not been able to take in positive emotional learning from the affects of primary adults may be both hypervigilant to adult affects and likely to read adult affects negatively at school. They may lack the awareness of why they are feeling the way that they do, as well as what to do to express complex emotions as part of a social narrative. Relationships with peers are often problematic as well, as children may project their own negative self-image onto others and feel that classmates are a threat.

Object Constancy and the Ability to Self-Comfort

Well-supported children whose experiences with adults weigh on the side of the positive most often reach the milestone of object constancy in older toddlerhood, between 28 and 36 months of age. Once object constancy is attained, children are able to hold their attachment partners "in mind and heart" even when they are physically separate. Separation reactions become less extreme, as the attachment partner becomes internally accessible.

The milestone of object constancy frees children to become less preoccupied with parental presence and absence, and more available for deep involvement in exploration and learning. Once children have reached this milestone, there is often a leap in the development of symbolic processes, empowering more complex language and play, and leading to the drive for mastery. "Why?" may be the child's new favorite word, as cause-and-effect relationships are discovered and explored.

At School. Typically developing children who come to school with object constancy not only are likely to weather the storms of separation more readily, but have a readiness for meeting the social challenges of group life. Object constancy allows children to survive the many moments of adversity that are certain to happen in the early childhood setting. Children who carry an internal connection to a primary adult who is loving and reliable has an internal source of comfort to draw on when another child grabs a toy, draws on their paper, or declares that they are "not my friend!" Young children may still require some support from the teacher in order to resolve these moments favorably, but the children with object constancy *know* that they are worthy of comfort and therefore can reach out to the teacher or accept and integrate adult support when it is given. Once the attuned teacher is attentive, the problem can resolve, and the two former adversaries are found skipping hand in hand 10 minutes later.

Children who come to school without object constancy cannot tolerate the moments of adversity that are likely to come their way in an early childhood peer group. If they have not had consistent and supportive caregiving experiences with primary adults, there may be no comforting image for them to internalize to bring to school. In school, these children often feel alone and unsafe. When moments of adversity occur, they don't even seem to know that the teacher is in the room! Feeling alone, they react as though they *are* alone and often respond with aggressive force that seems out of proportion to what has actually transpired.

Without an internal source of comfort, and without the feeling that they are in the company of a trusted adult, children without object constancy may wreak havoc in the classroom. Without support for this milestone, behavior can become less tenable for teachers to contain as children grow. There is almost always a secondary social and emotional backlash to persistently inappropriate or aggressive behavior, resulting in children being deprived of joyful experience, being yelled at, being removed from the classroom, being ostracized by peers or being removed from the school, deepening the children's negative self-image and heightening the persistent sense of being alone and dispensable in a threatening world.

Cause and Effect and the Question "Why?"

As pointed out above, once children attain object constancy, they are more free to explore their environment and have the mental energy that allows them to learn from their explorations. When children have been well supported and well protected, and experiences have been fairly consistent and predictable, children become fascinated by their own impact on the environment. They begin to make connections between actions and outcomes, motivating their play choices and delighting in their own abilities to make things happen. Children at this age become very curious about cause-and-effect relationships that are not directly observable. The question "Why?" follows most statements made by adults. When parents and caregivers answer in simple ways that build on children's prior knowledge and experiences, children begin to put "two and two" together, feeding perceptually based intelligence and the development of cause-and-effect relationships.

Children learn that most things happen for a reason, and look for ways to understand how things work and why things happen. This developmental milestone stimulates young children's sense of wonder, enhances the foundation for conceptual development, and allows them to feel more secure during familiar transitions as well as weathering the storm of bigger changes.

At School. When children come to school with an experience-based conviction that there are reasons why things happen, cause-and-effect relationships are anticipated, and there is a developmental foundation for cognitive mastery as well as reciprocal social interaction and emotional security. Children feel safer when they can anticipate the course of events, and the ripple effects of those events. For example, a cloudy and windy walk to school may be a hint that rain might fall later in the day, and rain might prevent outdoor recess.

Looking for answers to small problems becomes second nature when children assume that there are cause-and-effect relationships to discover. Children who have had adult scaffolding to discover ways of mastering work with initially challenging materials, solve social dilemmas, or figure out and articulate what makes them feel sad or angry come to the classroom with a backpack full of skills that empower learning and social interaction.

It is extremely difficult for children to learn to appreciate cause-and-effect relationships if life has been unpredictable, erratic, gratuitously violent, or full of overwhelming, unanticipated events. When children have little opportunity to experience a sense of agency, see patterns in relationship between their actions and subsequent outcomes, or experience adults as acting intentionally and consistently, they may not be able to appreciate cause-and-effect relationships or think to question "Why?" in school. When they and their families experience social discrimination resulting in negative consequences without apparent cause, there may be no expectation that life can make sense. Although children who cannot appreciate cause-and-effect relationships may seem to master rote learning, once problem solving, inference, and scientific inquiry are called for, they are often at a loss. In addition, social issues and emotional distress can result when children are not attuned to the cause and effect of social dynamics in the classroom.

School is a good place for children to have another opportunity to learn about cause-and-effect relationships by experiencing a sense of agency and active discovery of their own abilities to make an impact through project work. Predictable routines that include meaningful dialogue about what makes children feel both positive and negative emotions, what causes children to feel hurt or left out, and the experience of natural consequence can create an infrastructure for understanding cause and effect. That infrastructure allows children to build their problem-solving skills as well as formulate questions about what they see and hear.

Dramatic Play

When young children move from solitary symbolic play to shared symbolic play with peers, children who are well protected from media overexposure begin to cocreate play narratives based on shared symbols of developmental and life experience issues. These cocreated dramatic play scenarios help children integrate and make sense of both the world around them and their own feeling states within a social context. Dramatic play has many critical functions in childhood. It promotes self-regulation and social flexibility while decreasing social and emotional isolation. It is the perfect recipe for the foundations of childhood mental health!

When young children are overexposed to media, they may use all of their dramatic play time to reenact things that they have seen and heard that are not yet fully processed. The images and emotional tone of the online material may be overwhelming, and thus need to be played about in an attempt to make emotional sense of what the children have taken in. In addition, the popular movies and videos made for children confer a kind of group membership status for the children who have seen them, and give children a ready-made script for dramatic play scenarios. Sadly, these scripts can distract children from creating their own play narratives.

At School. Given the enormous developmental benefits of dramatic play for toddlers, preschool children, prekindergarteners, kindergarteners, and children in the early grades, it is critical that early childhood programs value and foster this essential symbolic capacity. Schools that are informed by ERP make time and space for dramatic play and integrate the play into literacy, social studies, and art for children in the early elementary grades. This multiyear focus on play often seems counterintuitive to school leaders and parents who feel pressure for an early academic focus. However, schools that are committed to supporting the developmental motivations of children partner with them to help make sense of life experience. Play becomes a well-guarded resource to help their students with this mission. Although children's lives outside of school are often imagined to be full of unstructured time and open-ended play, this is rarely the case in 21st-century America. Teachers find children less capable of self-generated play themes, social flexibility, and creative narrative as outside of school time is either spent on electronic devices or in structured after-school activities. Paradoxically, school might be the only place that can offer appropriate opportunities for play skills to develop and flourish.

Developmental Phases of Friendship

Young children develop within the context of relationship, leaning, and depending on their primary attachment relationships with adults as the foundation for social and emotional growth. Motivation for, and quality of, relationships with other children may gradually become salient within the context of sibling dynamics, or within the early care or early childhood setting, changing incrementally as children mature. Relationships with peers look very different in toddlerhood, early childhood, elementary grades, and middle school grades, as children move through developmental pathways that lead to gradual emergence of a self that can connect with others in friendship.

The concept of friendship itself has been losing essential value in recent years as parents and teachers often refer to groups of young children as "friends," instead of "children," or "kids." Yet, it is important to look at peer relationships on a developmental continuum, in order to appreciate where children are within their peer group, and to support the emergence of meaningful peer relationships at different ages and stages (Rawlings, 1992).

Young toddlers may be engaged by seeing or being with other young toddlers, delighting in pointing and labeling their peer as "baby," as though looking in a mirror and finding that there is a familiar image looking back. Children at this age often interact through imitative sound making, touch, and physical exploration, resulting in both squeals of delight as well as sudden tearful cries. Since children this age lack self-other boundaries, physical explorations and expressions of affections can suddenly become hurtful. A kiss can become a bite without intent to do harm. Parents and teachers know that they need to remain close by when babies or young toddlers are together, so that interactions can be supervised and comfort can be given when needed.

Older toddlers (24–36 months) may be simultaneously attracted to peers and wary of their intentions, as the need to oppose and possess ("no" and "mine") dominates. Playing alongside others is appealing, as long as there is no demand to share toys. Two-year-olds are often aware that the other child involved in a struggle for ownership needs to be appeased and may offer them another toy to hopefully quell their desire for the coveted item. When engaged in outdoor play, older toddlers enjoy running and tumbling with one another, getting caught up in the collective joyful energy of group interaction. Two-year-olds might hold hands, skip, hug, and engage in play routines and thoroughly enjoy each other's company until someone falls down or sees another playful activity that looks like fun. Two-year-olds can show preferences for play partners, but when compromise is demanded, the partnership might not endure.

Three-year-olds who have been well protected and well supported have newfound mental energy for exploring their impact on the environment and observing cause-and-effect relationships. They are drawn to playing near other children, engaged in parallel discoveries of cause-and-effect relationships as they interact with materials within a social context.

Young 3-year-olds may have little tolerance for others intruding on their play and may require adult intervention to resolve conflicts that arise. Children at age 3 develop stronger preferences for play partners and can use their newly acquired object constancy to better weather adverse interactive moments.

At age 4, there is often a change in the motivation and meaning of peer relationships. Seemingly overnight, children become obsessed with peer approval. They may be compelled to ask one another "Are you my friend?" multiple times each day, often yearning to *have* a friend before knowing how to *be* a friend. Children at this age generally believe that they can only have one friend at a time and therefore answer "no" while they are in process of playing with one partner when another child asks the powerful question. The third child is likely to dissolve into tears, devastated that their invitation for friendship was rejected, although they have most likely reacted the same way earlier that same morning.

These friendship issues often persist through kindergarten, where children may become more adept at managing social nuances, more able to nurture friendships that they are motivated to keep, and more aware of the power that their acceptance or rejection of others has within the peer community.

By 1st grade, generally speaking, there are differences that emerge in friendship styles among boys and among girls. Dynamics of friendships among the girls become more dependent on an emerging, increasingly complex web of social narratives, while friendship connections among boys often become organized around shared interests.

By the time girls reach 2nd grade, there is usually a preference for identifying as "best friends" and a feeling of social isolation if a best friend cannot be found. Little boys may also have best friends but are generally comfortable with the feeling of belonging within an interest-based group. Social isolation may become a persistent feeling if there is no felt common ground to facilitate the sense of belonging in group life.

Children between the ages of 6 and 9 increasingly crave a sense of belonging and fairness in peer group interactions. As they become more invested in life apart from family, develop interests and talents, and become part of several aspects of group life, deeper, more stable, and more differentiated friendships may ensue.

Once puberty happens, peer dynamics become infused with the energy of romantic possibility. Since girls most often enter puberty before their male counterparts, their friendship dyads and circles in upper elementary grades may entertain themselves with playful preparation for romantic encounters and social fantasies about love and sex. Girls who don't feel ready to build this bridge to their future selves may feel self-conscious and seek friendships with other girls who are feeling the same. If girls haven't been well protected, their fantasies may be actualized in detrimental ways in premature sexual exploration or victimization.

When boys hit puberty, their friendship circles or dyads often hold the experiences of physical changes and hormonally charged sexual desires that ensue. The insecurities that often accompany these physiological changes can be masked by bravado and competitive attitude.

Since puberty is a time of personal change and identity-seeking that ripples throughout the peer community of upper elementary, middle school, and high school–aged children, social and emotional vulnerability is high. This vulnerability is heightened for LGBTQ+ teens who must integrate emergent identities that might be demeaned within their former friendship circles.

The need for friendships and friendship circles that can accept and hold diverse elements of sexual and person identity is crucial in order for young teens to thrive. Support for integration of multiple identities, such as gender, race, culture, and other aspects of historical and future self is enhanced when teens can go through this process of integration within a community of peers.

At School. School is usually the place where children's peer networks develop. Although schoolchildren may have outside opportunities for peer connection, these opportunities are not universal. Cultural attitudes about friendships in childhood vary, with some cultures encouraging play dates apart from school connections and other cultures depending on family networks for social opportunities.

Teachers are aware that peer dynamics matter and often strive to facilitate positive interactions between the children within their classroom communities. One popular way of doing this is by acknowledging acts of kindness or offering rewards for sharing or being tolerant. Although emphasizing kindness is hard to argue with, it is rarely an effective facilitator of peer-focused social development if enacted without consciousness of developmental process. For example, if teachers of very young children are putting all of their energies into trying to get their 2-year-old participants to share, they will always be at odds with the children, whose developmental mission is to own. If preschool teachers constantly refer to children as friends, whether or not they are actually interested in connecting with one another, it becomes more difficult to sort out and articulate their emergent understanding of friendship.

Without understanding the developmental reality of 4- and 5-year-old friendships, teachers will often respond to children's complaints about someone "not wanting to be my friend," with a reassuring statement such as, "We're all friends here in kindergarten." Since underlying developmental issues surrounding friendship are rarely acknowledged or addressed in the classroom, children soon come to the conclusion that authentic expression on friendship issues are unwanted in school. Therefore, they may increasingly maintain a dual reality when interacting with peers as they move through the elementary school grades. This may involve following classroom interaction rules including being kind while in the teacher's presence, and acting out the complex and often-negative parts of peer dynamics in the cafeteria, playground, bathroom, or other out-of-classroom venues.

Sadly, negative peer dynamics that evolve when no adults are present can have a life of their own, leaving socially vulnerable children to become targets of other children's negative feelings unprotected. As children get older and more sophisticated about technology, they may retreat to the virtual world to share their anger, hurt, and rage.

Paradoxically, allowing only positive feelings and actions *within* the classroom can force the negative feelings and dynamics that develop between children to go underground, but linger just below the surface, ready to erupt when supervision is absent. In more extreme cases, schools may vilify unkind words and behavior as bullying, often isolating the children who are labeled as bullies. These are often the children who are the most overwhelmed by negative experiences and the least able to find a place for their negative feelings to live without getting them into trouble. Risk factors for these children build as they move through the grades if they are seen through the lens of "good and bad," instead of through the lenses of development and experience.

Power Versus Powerlessness

At ages 4, 5, and 6, children become cognitively astute enough to determine that relative to adults, they don't have very much power. They are little in a big world, and this realization brings a developmental leaning toward a feeling of powerlessness. In order to compensate for feeling small, children at this age are compelled to identify with powerful figures. Superheroes, royalty, and other characters of strength and status who are even more powerful than a child's own parents are tremendously appealing. Children are driven to prove their own strength and tend to become very competitive with one another. Being first, tallest, fastest, and strongest feels essential. Being the winner in every game supports the child's identity as a victorious conqueror.

When spending time with 4-, 5-, and 6-year-olds, it is easy to conclude that they are feeling a little *too* powerful, until the collapse of the compensatory identity is revealed by the devastated reaction to losing the board game, being second in line, or being outrun by another child. Worries about body integrity increase, and concerns about bumps, bruises, and other "boo-boos" require many Band-Aids and much adult reassurance to keep feelings of powerlessness at bay.

At School. It is crucial for educators and school policymakers to understand the developmental conflict of power versus powerlessness. This is not only helpful for understanding children's behavior in pre-K and the early grades, but is essential to understanding the importance of developmentally accessible curriculum in preschool, kindergarten, and 1st grade. When curriculum is on the "just-right" developmental level for children in this age group, children's classroom discoveries and connections become empowering, and learning becomes a source of powerful feelings. "Look what I did!," "Look what I found!," and "Look what I made!" are indications that young children feel empowered by their learning. Challenges that are on the just-right developmental level or within the *zone of proximal development* can extend capacity in confident, engaged learners (Vygotsky, 1980). When teacher–child relationships are supportive, and learning is engaging and allows for mastery at multiple levels, a stage for lifelong learning is being set.

When curriculum is not in sync with the developmental levels of the children in the room, schools run an enormous risk of engendering children's feelings of powerlessness in the classroom. When curriculum feels inaccessible, children at this age can become overwhelmed by feelings of inadequacy. When this happens, they may do anything they can to avoid academic demands. This allergy to learning is hard to cure and may become a persistent deterrent to academic progress. Fighting for accessible and meaningful curriculum for early childhood and early grade classrooms has become an essential and frequently misunderstood mission for professionals who want the best outcomes for children.

Fantasy and Reality

Very young children cannot differentiate fantasy from reality and cannot predict outcomes in realistic ways. Therefore, mandated adult-to-child ratios for toddler care are much lower than preschool or kindergarten ratios. Because toddlers cannot yet predict outcomes, they are compelled to test reality to find out what will happen. The familiar "No, no! Don't touch!" can give very young children pause before touching the hot stove or putting their finger in the electrical outlet. Little by little, well-supported, well-protected children begin to internalize parental warnings, and begin to appreciate cause-and-effect relationships.

Although children younger than 7 still blend perceptual intelligence with emergent concepts to explain what they see and hear, as they approach the age of 5, most children are beginning to draw some lines between real and pretend. For example, Superman can fly without an airplane in the video, but children pretending to be Superman can only pretend to fly. A cartoon character in a computer game can shoot creatures and cause them to evaporate, but if a child found a gun and shot at a real animal, the animal would die.

When preschool and school-aged children cannot differentiate between fantasy and reality, and cannot predict realistic consequences of their actions, their supervision needs remain higher than what is typically provided. These children might test reality in ways similar to toddlers, but, being taller and stronger and not as well supervised, they can seriously injure themselves or other children if acting in fantasy mode without the ability to predict actual consequences.

At School. It is important to look at children's capacity to make degrees of differentiation between reality and fantasy once children are enrolled in early grade programs. Without staff awareness, children who have not developed the capacity to differentiate real and pretend or predict logical consequences of their actions, are especially vulnerable to acting out or exploring in dangerous ways when apart from their classroom teacher. The lunchroom, play yard, hallway, bathroom, or school bus may lack the protective capacity to keep such children safe without additional attention to their activities.

ASSESSING POTENTIAL TO NURTURE LEARNING

Our public schools are obsessed with assessing children, and our school districts are obsessed with assessing individual schools on the basis of those child-assessment outcomes. In recent years, assessments of classroom interactions and social environments have been added to the mix. However, it is rare to see information harvested from those assessments being used to promote a deeper understanding of the ways that child development issues come to school. It is rare to see school systems supporting staff to be aware of the meaning and power of their own developmental partnerships with children. When stress and anxiety dominate the classroom climate, it is rare to see a change of pace that decreases pressure and allows for deeper exploration in learning.

When educators perceive their mandate as being accountable to the children in front of them by looking through the lens of development, children and adults feel the difference when they walk into the classroom. When schools commit to supporting the developmental needs of the children in their communities, they are guided by a powerful and complex professional knowledge base that is aligned with children's own process of finding meaning in what they learn. This approach to teaching and learning needs a voice as least as loud as the powerful forces who promote Common Core Standards and rigidly enforce score-driven practice without taking children and teachers into account. Since the inventors and promoters of score-driven practice have, by and large, never been in a classroom, the voice of reason must come from inside the field.

Looking Through the Lens of Experience

Child development is, in part, experience dependent in order to unfold in optimal ways. Each child brings a life of experiences to school every morning, and those experiences can provide a wealth of opportunities for teaching and learning. Educators may be familiar with *funds of knowledge* research and practice, which recommends tapping into children's diverse fountains of experienced-based, preexisting competence as a foundation for academic learning at school (Gonzalez et al., 2005). Inviting life experience stories into the classroom also provides teachers with a window into their students' lives outside of school, allowing teachers to more effectively partner with children who struggle to make sense of their small worlds.

Historically, teachers have been discouraged from looking through the lens of experience. Traditionalists forbid teachers from sharing information about children from one grade to the next, encouraging teachers to see each child as a blank slate, erasing the knowledge gained by an attuned teacher the year before. These schools rarely engage parents in dialogues about their children, but rather inform parents about expectations and curriculum without gaining much insight from parents in the process.

Yet traditional schools tend to have more moderate attitudes about acknowledging children's life experience than "no excuses" charter schools. Many of these charter schools operate on the philosophy that acknowledging difficult life experiences will lessen expectations for success. These schools appear to be unfamiliar with the science of childhood adversity, which points to the power of life experience to both enhance and diminish developmental outcomes (Darling-Hammond et al., 2020; Shonkoff & Garner, 2011).

When children's life experiences are ignored in the classroom, children with intense life experience stories are alone with the task of making emotional sense of what they carry for hours every day. Intense high-stress experience can be terribly distracting, prevent focused attention, intrude on memory, and hinder the learning process, and children with burdensome experience are often left alone to feel overwhelmed and inadequate at school. Since some children have a limited capacity to hold internal distress, they may act out aspects of their painful experiences in interactions with other children as well as with authority figures, compounding their issues when teachers and other children react negatively.

LIFE EXPERIENCES AND THE DEVELOPING BRAIN

The field of brain research has given us insight into the ways that a baby's brain develops in response to interaction with adult caregivers. As pointed out in Chapter 2, connections within the brain wake up and become active when joyful, reciprocal interactions occur within attachment relationships. These relationships both stimulate cognition and provide a protective space for young children to develop without becoming overwhelmed by the big world. When children are surrounded by adults who are able to engage in this way, the brain has the ingredients that it needs to thrive. Neurons in the brain are busy creating synapsis and building connections between them (Owens & Tanner, 2017; Tierney & Nelson, 2009). When life is unforgivingly stressful for the adults in the child's mini-universe, making them less available and less able to engage in reciprocal dialogue, the young child's brain is left thirsting for at least one adult who can provide this crucial form of cognitive, social, and emotional nurture. Young children are wired for reciprocal social interaction, but are partner dependent in order to "set the wheels in motion" (National Scientific Council on the Developing Child, 2020). If no adult partner emerges who can engage in the early affective dialogue, or if trauma or loss disrupts or fractures the dialogue, developmental ripple effects become evident as the child grows. The child entering school may present as disorganized, inattentive, lacking self-regulation, aggressive, or out of sync. He may seem to be at a loss to make sense of the curricular material being presented.

Although the child who presents with these issues soon gets on the radar of school staff, the child's life story may remain hidden, and his need for adult partnership as a precursor for healthy socialization and empowered learning may go unseen. Children who need more contact with supportive adults frequently act in ways that annoy or anger the very adults with whom they need to connect. Children's difficult behavior may distract the adults at school from providing an essential ingredient for academic success a relationship with a responsive adult. Although research finds the infant brain to require nurturing, reciprocal interaction in order to thrive, it also emphasizes the plasticity of the human brain to respond to these nurturing relationships *throughout childhood*. Although constant assessment and behavior charts cannot repair brain function, relationship-based practice has the capacity to offer a healing process for children.

THE MASK OF BEHAVIOR

A school can feel under siege when more than a few children are unable to contain their rage, sadness, grief, loneliness, or fears in the classroom. Disruptive, aggressive, and explosive behaviors terrify other children, exhaust teachers, and overwhelm school resources to respond while managing the everyday needs of a school community. Behavior often becomes "the dragon" that a school tries to "slay" with weapons of rewards' systems, withholding of pleasurable experience, disciplinary codes, and, in many settings, suspension. Banishing difficult behavior is thought to be the ultimate goal leading to the victory of an environment that lets "good kids" learn. When behavior becomes so overwhelming that it cannot be contained within the classroom or school building, children may be referred to more specialized settings.

Frequently, the specialized settings employ the same or similar behavior-focused strategies within a much smaller group of children. When on-site counseling or therapy is provided in school, clinicians may reach out to families to try to get a better understanding of children's life experiences, but may be discouraged from addressing issues that go beyond or underlie children's behavior in the classroom.

THE VALUE OF LIFE STORY: A CORE CONCEPT OF EMOTIONALLY RESPONSIVE PRACTICE

In many early childhood and elementary grade programs, the life experience stories that children carry into their classrooms are whispered by older children to one another, known by the school aid who lives next door to a difficult child's family, or written down in the school social worker's files that are sealed by the oath of confidentiality. When children don't behave, pay attention, retain learning, or communicate well, they may eventually be referred for evaluation. Very often, these evaluations include taking children's psychosocial history, as well as a speech and language evaluation, an occupational therapy (OT) evaluation, and psychological and educational testing. When support services are recommended as a result, the psychosocial stories are rarely addressed. Speech and language, OT, and behavior support may be suggested, as though the child's developmental struggles exist entirely apart from her psychosocial story.

In contrast, Emotionally Responsive Practice (ERP) schools value psychosocial stories and use them to inform routines, school practices, and curriculum. ERP assumes that if the resolution of foundational developmental milestones is in part experience dependent, it becomes essential to evaluate children *in light of* their prior and current experiences! In order to answer the question "has this child had the prior experiential support needed for mastery of these milestones?" educators must do their best to become informed about prior experiences. Otherwise, they are evaluating children's developmental status and learning status *as though poor outcomes indicate poor potential.* Looking through the lens of experience as well as through the lens of development can provide a more complete view of a child's status, as well as a blueprint for meaningful support and hopeful outcomes.

When the developmental milestones elaborated in Chapter 2 are considered with children's life experiences in mind, the interaction between development and experience becomes clear. Attachment, differentiation, psychological home base, the birth of symbolic process, autonomy, object constancy, appreciation of cause and affect, peer relationships and the balance of power, and powerlessness are all experience dependent in order to resolve well. Those developmental issues may look very different in children who have experienced loss, disruption, homelessness, trauma, and other significant events during the time when these essential developmental processes are unfolding.

Even positive events can create disequilibrium and temporary developmental regression in children. For example, the birth of a baby can create ambivalent feelings in the child who was the youngest before the new addition to the family arrived. There is excitement about the new baby, often accompanied by feelings of loss and jealousy. Young children in this situation want to identify with their parents' joy, and can easily express their sense of wonder and feelings of affection for the tiny baby, but sometimes can't find a way to express their feelings of loss or anger. Teachers of preschool children see and hear children's ambivalence about their new siblings in their behavior and play. The pre-K child who kisses his baby sister on the head before separating from their parent may then run to the doll corner and fling a baby doll across the room. At rest time he asks for a pacifier because the new baby has one, and it isn't fair that he doesn't.

Teachers in healing schools listen to the stories that parents and children tell or show, whether the communication is verbal, written, through play or drawing or through behavioral expression. Humans most often respond to stories with empathy (Barton & Garvis, 2019). Both children and adults begin to identify with experiences that are shared in the form of story. Story sharing has the capacity for enhancing empathy in the listener, and diminishing feelings of guilt and isolation in the storyteller. For example, the pre-K teacher who knows that many of the children in her class have had the experience of the birth of a younger sibling may welcome story sharing among the children about becoming a big brother or sister. She makes sure that children have invitations to express ambivalent feelings about their baby siblings within the safety of the classroom. Although children's behavior can be trying as they adjust to this change in family constellation, having been in the field for years and having seen similar reactions play out before, the teacher is in a good position to use what she knows about development and life experience to encourage constructive expression around this life-altering event.

Story as Blueprint for Emotionally Responsive Practice

Clio, the teacher in the pre-K classroom mentioned above, reads to the children every day before lunch. She chooses the book *Julius, Baby of the World* as her read-aloud, knowing that the story reflects the main character's negative and positive feelings about having a new baby at home (Henkes, 1990). She invites Josh, the child whose baby sister was born most recently, to sit next to her while she reads. Once the story begins to unfold, Clio notices a heightened level of attention from several children in the group, including Josh. When she has finished reading the book, she asks the group what the story reminds them of. Several children talk about their own experiences of becoming big brothers and sisters. One child says, "I like my baby brother, but sometimes he cries all day, and I wish he would go away!" Josh beamed. Another child said, "When my baby came to live in my house, I was the best helper! But one day I asked my mommy if we could give him back to the hospital and she said no, because he is ours forever." Josh breathed a sigh of relief.

Clio invited the children to draw and dictate their own stories about babies if they wanted to. She also offered to engage interested children in a baby study, including remembering about what they liked and needed when they were babies, as well as figuring out what babies can do and what they need. Several children were interested, including Josh, whose regressive behavior diminished once he was able to connect to peers who shared his ambivalent feelings.

Clio's colleague Molly taught kindergarten in the same public school. Five-year-old Miles entered Molly's classroom midyear. He seemed unfamiliar with a classroom setting and was generally disorganized. Molly was feeling overwhelmed by having a new child enter her class after the children had finally settled in, but she was generally a warm and nurturing teacher and did her best to welcome Miles. He showed fleeting interest in classroom materials, exploring many things but never really staying with anything. Miles's main focus at school was initially on food. He ate mountains of snacks and always needed to be reminded that lunch would be served as well. Although he didn't seem ready for, or interested in, the academic curriculum that the school district required, he did use his energy to track his teacher's every move, seemingly anxious that she might disappear.

Molly's school used Story Gathering (Koplow, 2002) during the initial parent–teacher conference to learn the important stories of each child's life. Molly called Miles's home to schedule the Story-Gathering Conference a few weeks after he arrived. Miles's foster mother came to the conference and let Molly know what she knew about Miles's story. She had no early developmental history, since she met Miles when he was 4, but she knew that he was in foster care because of parental substance abuse. She knew that Miles and his little brothers had been found alone at home with no food or electricity. She knew that Miles was vigilant about caring for his younger brothers, who were also in the foster home. The foster mother also shared her own doubts about being able to care for the three children for more than a few months, because Miles's 2-year-old brother was always running away when they went outside, and the foster mother felt she was too elderly to keep up with him.

Molly knew enough about development to know that if Miles's earlier life had been similar to his life at the time of foster placement, Miles was likely to need partnership to support earlier milestones, as well as to help him make sense of his life in the present. Molly used Miles's story to inform her interactions with him, inform her classroom routines, and infuse her curriculum with meaningful content. She was warm and nurturing with every child, but worked hard to build a supportive bond with Miles, inviting him to check in when he first arrived in the morning, and before he left at the end of the day. She wanted to support Miles's ability to use the classroom as a psychological home base. She let Miles and the other children know where she was going if she left the room for a few minutes, and let them know when she would be back. She forecast any changes in routine and held Miles's hand when the class was invited to join an assembly or went to another classroom for music.

When the class was studying family, Molly made literacy choices that included books about foster families, as well as books about having younger brothers and sisters. Although Miles rarely sat still for very long, and was usually inattentive during storytime, he was riveted by the stories that reflected his own. Molly frequently invited the children to draw something about the stories that she read aloud, and asked them to dictate or write a narrative about what the story reminded them of. Miles usually quickly scribbled on the blank page, offering a single-word dictation that seemed unrelated to his drawing. After Molly read a book to the class about foster families, Miles drew himself and his two little brothers standing in between a big house and a tiny scribbled house. He dictated, "That's me."

Molly was delighted with Miles's progress. Over time, he began to seem more relaxed, more interested in the curriculum, and more focused when he was able to relate to content. His drawings and dictations were becoming thoughtful and elaborate. He was able to find Molly when he needed help, which allowed him to stay regulated enough to begin to be social and playful with other children. When it was time for Miles to transition to 1st grade, Molly persuaded her principal to place him with the most nurturing 1st-grade teacher LaShawn. Molly knew that Miles would continue to need relationship-based practice as he moved through the grades in order to thrive. Because her school leader believed in relationship-based practice, Molly was optimistic about Miles's future at the school.

Hear No Evil: Avoiding Story; Avoiding Children

Sadly, at the end of the summer between 1st and 2nd grade, Miles's foster mother's prediction that she would be unable to keep up with the children in the long run came true. Miles and his brothers were placed in another foster home that was a good distance from his school. He was then enrolled in the zoned school closer to his new foster placement. Concerned, his previous teachers, Molly and LaShawn, asked their school social worker to call Miles's new 2nd-grade teacher, explain his situation, school progress, ongoing need for support, and forecast the likelihood that he would be reacting to the loss of a supportive foster mother and a supportive school environment.

This zoned school was in the same district as the school Miles had attended but had a very different approach to teaching. The 2nd-grade teacher told the social worker that she was "not interested" in knowing too much about her students. Knowing too much might distract her from her mission of preparing her children for the 3rd grade, which was a testing grade. She mentioned her success using behavior charts to control difficult children. Molly and LaShawn felt sick when the school social worker related this conversation.

The first time that Miles's 2nd-grade teacher put his name on "Red" (poor behavior: loses privilege) on the classroom behavior chart, Miles had a tantrum in the classroom. The second time, he threw a chair at his teacher. After being suspended for 3 days, he returned looking sullen and depressed. Instead of doing his classwork, he drew a picture of a violent video game that his new older foster brother had shown him the night before. He was in his seat, but he was no longer present in the classroom.

Permission to Know

School leaders in Emotionally Responsive Practice schools give teachers permission to know what children are carrying in their minds and hearts when they come to school every day. Without "permission to know," even caring teachers remain ambivalent about "knowing too much" about the children who spend hours every day in their company. Without permission to know, teachers may not be aware that they are indeed living with and feeling the children's life stories every hour of every day, often without a verbal context for understanding. One 3rd-grade teacher, Ms. B, confided, "I finally understand why Nava has been so distracted and disengaged all semester! I overheard her tell her best friend that her parents are getting divorced. It's awkward, because now I know, but I'm 'not supposed to know.'"

When teachers feel "permission to know" what they have actually felt and taken in about children's lives, they can more effectively partner with children to support emotional well-being and learning. If Ms. B felt empowered "to know" Nava's story, she could have acknowledged it to Nava. She could have approached Nava and told her the truth. For example, "I overheard you talking about your parents divorcing. I know how hard that can be for kids, and how it can feel almost impossible to think about anything else." Nava might have gotten tearful, remained silent, or communicated more about what was happening for her. Her teacher could have acknowledged Nava's response and invited her to use her journal or other writing assignments to give her thoughts and feelings a voice. Had this happened, Nava would have known that she was not alone with her hurtful experience while she was in the classroom, and could then be more present by using literacy periods, drama, and family studies to express what she can't seem to get out of her mind, even when she is in school.

The Power of Stories Untold

Untold stories leave children alone with overwhelming and distracting reality and leave teachers in the dark to make sense of behavior that appears to be coming from nowhere. When children's difficult experiences have never been talked about, clarified, or put into a meaningful context by emotionally connected adults, children themselves may not be able to put their experiences into words. This is true for adolescents as well as for preschool children, and all of the ages in between.

When children are isolated with overwhelming experiences, without invitations to talk about them, draw about them, write about them, or play about them, emotions that are connected to these experiences are likely to erupt. Teachers that ask children why they are behaving in disruptive ways rarely get satisfying answers. Typically, the children themselves are not in touch with the social–emotional cause and effect that connect experience and behavior.

They are sometimes unable to name the issues that are fueling their emotional outbursts. Asking children why they are being uncooperative or disruptive is like asking children to put together a complex puzzle without making all of the pieces accessible. When adults in their everyday lives help them gather and acknowledge as many of the pieces as possible, children can feel safe enough to engage in a healing process that helps them to assemble a personal and social narrative, consolidate a positive sense of self, and begin to integrate cognitive, social, and emotional domains. The techniques suggested in Part II will help teachers to engage in supporting children in this important process of integration.

THE GOOD MIRROR AND OTHER TOOLS OF EMOTIONALLY RESPONSIVE PRACTICE

CHAPTER 4

Using Reflective Technique in School

Public schools that adopt the mission of supporting the mental health and learning potential of all children have the capacity to provide them with strong and positive adult–child relationships that give children a "good mirror" for development and experience. A good mirror is one that reflects accurately, affirming all kinds of experience as well as the whole range of human emotions in nonjudgmental ways. In order to provide a good mirror for schoolchildren, Emotionally Responsive Practice (ERP) teachers, school social workers, and school leaders look through the lens of child development, to view children within a developmental context and reflect a positive image back to them in developmentally meaningful ways.

In order to provide a good mirror for schoolchildren, ERP teachers, school social workers, and school leaders also look through the lens of children's life experiences in order to respect and reflect an accurate image of their experiential reality, so that they don't have to carry overwhelming experiences alone.

A good mirror acknowledges both children's positive and negative affects, and their positive and negative experiences, without valuing one over the other, while consistently reflecting a positive image of the children *themselves*. Teachers and school leaders are powerful figures in children's eyes. Children internalize their teacher's and school leader's thoughts and feelings about them. Teachers and school leaders who are good mirrors can buffer the impact of negative messages that children may receive from others. Without a good mirror coming from the adults that surround children at school, children may be more vulnerable to the "bad mirrors" (or "broken mirrors") that may come from other children, people in their outside lives, media, or society at large.

There are many classroom friendly reflective techniques that can be integrated into public school practice that have powerful and positive effects on children's well-being and engagement in learning. In this chapter these techniques will be described and explored within classroom-centered vignettes to demonstrate applicability.

REFLECTIVE LANGUAGE AS A "GOOD MIRROR"

The teaching profession demands that teachers "think on their feet." Teaching is an improvisational art as well as a science, as teachers respond to children's thoughts, feelings, actions, and reactions all day long, without necessarily being able to foresee what children will do or say at any given moment. Teachers have to become proficient at problem solving, multitasking, and "directing" the drama of classroom life at an impressive pace, rarely missing a beat even when several dynamics are occurring simultaneously.

ERP teachers add another skill to their repertoire of teacher–child interaction. This skill asks teachers and school leaders to stop and reflect on what is happening *before* giving directions or asking problem-solving questions. In addition, this skill requires teachers and school leaders to *first* reflect verbally on the essence of what has occurred, before asking or demanding anything from the child or children involved. Teachers listen to children's responses if responses are forthcoming, which may indicate that another reflective comment is needed or may indicate a more receptive state for a suggestion, approach, or limit to be given.

Reflective language is distinctive for its unique communicative intent. Rather than language that reminds children to listen to the teacher or to follow rules, reflective language allows children to see and hear *themselves* during overwhelming emotional moments. Children who are very upset often lose touch with themselves and with the adult who is trying to help. When adults make reflective comments in nonjudgmental ways, these comments draw the child in and become the verbal equivalent of providing an actual mirror that reflects the child and the teacher together in that moment. Verbal mirrors, like physical mirrors, can help center the child in the present, especially if a child's reaction or behaviors are related to past experience.

Without practice, reflective language can feel unnatural or counterintuitive. It takes time to use it with ease. At first, reflective language may seem strangely passive, unnatural, or disingenuous. However, once reflective language becomes second nature to the educator, it can be a powerful tool of communication and support throughout the school day.

Using Reflective Language at School

Reflective language can be used with children to communicate perceptions, affirm children's actual and emotional experiences, and bring children and teacher into a shared space. Consider the following three examples of applied reflective language:

Elias. A pre-K child, Elias, is refusing to enter the classroom. He is sitting in his cubby with his elbows on his knees and his head in his hands. Elias's fingers only partially hide his scowling face. All the other children have already entered the room with the classroom assistant, leaving the teacher Donna to assist Elias. Before learning to use reflective language, Donna would have tried to convince Elias to come in, or coax him with memories of happy times in the room, or threaten to take away appealing events. Instead, Donna begins the dialogue with reflective language.

> *Donna:* Elias, you look like you really don't want to come into the classroom today!
> *Elias:* (Looks up at Donna and shakes his head.)
> *Donna:* I think shaking your head is another way to say "no."
> *Elias:* No stupid classroom! No hurting! (Elias pouts after speaking.)
> *Donna:* It sounds like you are remembering one of our classroom rules, "No hurting." You don't look happy about that!
> *Elias* (angrily): Because Ian hit me on the bus! Mama said, "If Ian hits you, hit him back!" The classroom says, "No hurting." (Elias's arms are now folded across his chest revealing his angry scowl and tears that haven't yet fallen.)
> *Donna:* Oh! I see! You look really sad and angry about that! Mama said one thing, and we say something else at school! I think Ian needs to know that hitting hurt you, and you didn't like it!
> *Elias:* (Looks up at Donna, nodding.)
> *Donna:* (Holds out her hand to Elias.) Since there's no hurting in the classroom, let's go talk to Ian about what happened on the bus, and let him know how you're feeling! We better talk to the bus driver and the matron about "no hurting" on the bus! I will talk to Mama about our school rules.
> *Elias:* (Stands up and takes Donna's hand and they go into the classroom.)

Luis and Fernando. Two recent arrivals in Anya's 1st-grade class, Luis and Fernando, have been brought back to the room during recess by a school aid, who angrily tells Anya that the boys have been fighting, calling them troublemakers in Spanish and letting them know that they are being brought back to Anya because the principal was not in his office.

Fernando is crying so loudly that Anya can hardly hear the playground aid's story. Luis proceeds to pace back and forth, cursing in Spanish and punching his leg with his fist. Anya sends the school aid back to the playground. In a calm, empathic voice, Anya begins the reflective dialogue.

>*Anya:* It seems like something happened on the playground that made both of you very upset!

(Fernando continues to weep, and Luis looks up at Anya for a second, continuing to pace but at a slower pace.)

>*Anya:* Ms. Juana was talking about fighting.
>*Luis:* (in a low voice) The big boy took Fernando's hat!
>*Anya:* The big boy took your hat, Fernando?

(Fernando nods, wiping his eyes, still convulsing.)

>*Luis:* I tried to get the hat for Fernando, but the big boy punched me here! (Luis pointed to his stomach.) Then Fernando punched the big boy! Then Ms. Juana was yelling, and Fernando was afraid.
>*Anya:* I understand what happened now. A big boy took Fernando's hat and Luis tried to help and get the hat back, but the big boy punched Luis! Then Fernando tried to help Luis and punched the big boy.
>*Luis:* Si. But now Fernando is afraid because Ms. Juana told us we were in trouble with the principal. Fernando thinks maybe the principal will send us back to our country.
>*Anya:* (Motioning Fernando to come closer to her, and sit beside her.) I'm so sorry that Ms. Juana scared you, Fernando! I will tell her about the big boy, and about how you were trying to help each other. If the big boy has been in our school for a long time, he should know that there's no teasing or punching allowed on the playground! You guys are new to our school, so you might not know those rules. If a big boy takes your hat or hurts you, you can find Ms. Juana or another school aid and ask for help.
>*Luis:* (Nodding, translates what Anya had said in Spanish for Fernando, since he is not as fluent in English.)
>*Anya:* Tell Fernando that our principal Mr. D might remind children about the rules, but he never sends children away. (Luis does this, and Fernando's distressed affect melts into relief.) Both Mr. D and I are glad to have you with us in our school!

(Anya gives the boys crayons and paper and invites them to draw for the rest of the period.)

Layla and Kaitlyn. Two 5th-grade girls, Layla and Kaitlyn, have been summoned by the principal Heather after she received three distraught phone calls from parents of other girls in their classroom. These parents were naming Layla and Kaitlyn as "mean girls" who were influencing the other girls to exclude their children from group life both in and out of school. Two of the three girls had stayed at home, complaining of headaches and stomachaches the week before. Their mothers suspect that their anxiety about the mean girls was making them feel sick.

Heather welcomes the Layla and Kaitlyn into her office and has them sit down. The girls seem unfazed. Heather begins the reflective dialogue.

> *Heather:* Maybe you are wondering why I called for you today. I know you both are doing well in your schoolwork, and you both participate in a lot of school activities and look pretty happy about being here.

(The girls smile and nod.)

> *Heather:* On the other hand, there are at least three other girls in your class who are very unhappy in school, and their moms seem to think that you have something to do with that.

(Layla and Kaitlyn look at each other, then back at Heather. Layla looks stricken, while Kaitlyn shrugs her shoulders.)

> *Heather:* Maybe you can think of something that happened to make other girls in your class feel uncomfortable or unwanted.
> *Kaitlyn:* Well, I think some of the girls just don't like us. We never said anything mean to them! Maybe they wanted us to get in trouble!

(Layla is now crying silent tears and sniffing.)

> *Heather:* Layla, you look pretty upset. Are you remembering something that happened that Kaitlyn didn't mention?

(Layla nods her head and continues to cry.)

> *Heather:* OK. I will meet with each of you separately to see if we can come to an understanding about what's going on with the girls in your class. Before I do that, I want to tell you something while you are both here together. Telling other kids to say mean things, or to reject or exclude other girls makes those kids feel

that no one wants them here! Only *you* can decide whom *you* want to play with or hang out with, but you can't tell *other* kids whom to play with or hang out with. This means you can't try to influence their choices in person *or* through social media messages! *Everyone* in our community needs to feel comfortable and valuable at school, and when you tell other girls whom to include and whom to exclude, you are making the excluded girls feel so badly that they can't even come into the building! That can't continue to happen anymore in my school! That's not what this school is about!

(Both girls nod their heads to communicate that it won't happen anymore, Layla still crying and Kaitlyn looking tense and sullen.)

Heather sends Kaitlyn to the waiting room to first talk with Layla. Heather knows that Layla was likely following Kaitlyn's path to win her approval. She feels confident about helping Layla put her energy into more prosocial endeavors.

Heather knows that Kaitlyn's situation is more complicated. Kaitlyn has a lot of reasons to want to be in control of her world outside of home. Kaitlyn's older brother was addicted to opioids and has been in and out of rehab most of the last 2 years. Her dad was working two jobs to supplement what the health insurance paid for his son's treatment. Her mother has a demanding job as the director of a residence for disabled young adults. After a few more meetings, one with just Kaitlyn and another with Kaitlyn and the three girls, Heather plans to refer Kaitlyn to the school social worker for weekly counseling sessions.

Analysis of Reflective Dialogues

In each scenario described, the adult uses reflective language to address situations in which the children are reacting in ways that are counterproductive to the group's well-being. In the first scenario, Elias is resisting the routine, making it necessary for the classroom assistant to manage 17 children while his teacher Donna tries to assist him. Her verbally reflecting on his actions and affect without making initial demands increases his feeling of connection to Donna and allows him to engage in a productive dialogue, resulting in his ability to make the transition.

In the second scenario, Luis and Fernando are protecting each other by becoming physically aggressive with other children, which gets them into trouble on the playground while they are apart from the adults who know them well enough to know their stories. Reflective technique helps their teacher Anya stay with, and verbally reflect, the *boys'* experience of what happened, instead of simply mirroring the school aid's punitive attitude. This helps the boys to feel less afraid and less likely to be paralyzed by fight or flight reactivity. The nonjudgmental reflective dialogue creates a level of receptivity in the children that allows their teacher to eventually understand what happened, and mirror the cause and effect of the incident. She then is able to introduce the school's rules and resources, and reassure Fernando that his underlying fear about getting in trouble in school resulting in deportation will not happen. The information gained within the reflective dialogue carves a path for Anya to involve other key staff members in supporting children in Luis and Fernando's position more effectively within the school community. Specifically, Anya meets with the principal to discuss the children's fears and confusion about the role of authority figures at school and requests some SEL work for the playground monitors and school aids.

In the last scenario, 5th-graders Layla and Kaitlyn have been intentionally hurting other girls in ways that have escaped their teacher's attention and are antithetical to the embracing school climate that the principal Heather wants to foster. Heather felt terrible when she heard from parents that some 5th-grade girls were feeling so marginalized that they were becoming physically ill and staying out of school. After the second phone call, Heather began to feel enraged at these two girls, who were somehow able to undermine her mission to make the school a safe place. She took a breath and decided to wait a day before bringing them into the office, so that she could approach the issues more thoughtfully. She first spoke with the girl's teacher Rosalyn, who thought that the hurtful dynamics were being played out in the cafeteria and on the playground, and possibly through social media. Rosalyn also reminded her school leader about Kaitlyn's life outside of school, which had been revealed as part of the school's Story-Gathering practice.

The principal found this conversation enormously helpful. It gave her perspective as well as helping her with a plan of action. Her meeting with Layla and Kaitlyn would be the first intervention, which would be a reflective dialogue about what was happening, followed by clear communication of her own priorities about acceptance and inclusion. After the details had been sorted out, she planned to meet with the excluded group of girls with Layla and Kaitlyn present, using reflective language to begin a dialogue about group dynamics.

In addition to carrying out those plans, as described earlier, Heather asked the school social worker to be present in the cafeteria to meet with small groups of girls every day, and to be available to observe on the playground for a while as well. Heather let the children know that there would be new rules and new resources at lunchtime and outside time.

After spending time on the playground, the social worker suggested having more play equipment available to the kids, such as large rubber balls, jump ropes, and hula hoops. The social worker and principal designated one of the brick walls on the playground as a space for chalk drawings and writing suggestions for a safer school community. Fifth-graders would vote on the most interesting and effective images and would use art class time to paint them on the wall so that they would be there permanently.

In each of the above scenarios, reflective language was used as the initial tool to promote connection and understanding in communicating with children in difficult situations. Because this kind of communication often results in additional learning for the adult engaged in the process, the next steps vary widely according to what comes out of the process. For example, in the meeting involving Layla and Kaitlyn, Heather chooses to reflect Layla's distressed affect rather than reflecting Kaitlyn's statement denying their (her) role in the episode. Layla's tears are communicating the opposite of what Kaitlyn is saying, meaning that Heather feels Layla's tears express regret that she *had* been involved, and perhaps anxiety about being in trouble for doing something she shouldn't have done. Reflecting Layla's feelings takes the conversation in a more productive direction.

If the meeting had been with Kaitlyn only, Heather might have chosen to reflect Kaitlyn's statement of denial as well as the statement that she had heard from the distraught parents. For example, Heather might have said "It sounds like you are feeling like you and Layla were falsely accused of being involved with this, and at the same time, each of the three girls who were too upset to come to school told their moms that you and Layla were a part of it."

This reflective comment brings both sides into focus, communicating that both sides deserve attention and need resolution. Reflecting the child's point of view initially creates a less defensive posture, making it more likely that the child is able to take in what comes next.

REFLECTIVE LITERACY AS A "GOOD MIRROR"

Reflective literacy can also be used as a "good mirror" for children, resulting in multiple positive academic and social and emotional outcomes. For example, when teachers choose to read aloud from storybooks that reflect the developmental issues and life experiences of the children in the room, there is almost always heightened attention and engagement with the material (Koplow, 2002, 2007, 2008). Reflective literacy becomes a dialogue between children and their teachers, as well as among the children who comprise the group. When teachers share books that reflect the developmental issues and life experiences that children express in the classroom, children's responses to the reading then are used to inform the teachers' next literacy choices.

Reflective literacy, the process of choosing books that mirror children's issues through story, may initially feel counterintuitive to teachers. For instance, a 1st-grade teacher whose group of children grab things from one another may be inclined to read a book about sharing, to facilitate a more prosocial atmosphere. When a 6th-grade class moans about how overwhelming their homework assignments feel, their teacher may be inclined to choose a chapter book about a studious child who becomes a famous mathematician. Although these books may be valuable and motivating to some children, they essentially reflect the *teacher's* values and wishes instead of the children's. They reiterate a message children hear from their teachers and parents all day long, but this time in story form.

An ERP teacher using reflective literacy would look for books that mirror the *children's* issues and emotional experiences somewhere in the story. Instead of looking for a book entitled *The First Grade Learns to Share*, the ERP teacher might look for a book called *That's Mine!* Instead of looking for a book that extolled the value of hard work, the 6th-grade ERP teacher might look for a book about a kid who feels overwhelmed by schoolwork. These teachers may have the same ultimate goals as the more conventional teachers, meaning that they all want to improve dynamics and motivation in their classrooms. However, the ERP teachers have experienced the powerful ripple effect of an approach that offers children a good mirror for all kinds of feelings and all kinds of wishes, using the vehicles of story and metaphor to facilitate communication and deeper understanding. These powerful reflective books are not necessarily found in a separate section of the library! Many popular children's books that have stood the test of time are books that have captured timeless elements of children's development and experience. For example, *The Runaway Bunny, Where the Wild Things Are, The Very Hungry Caterpillar, Diary of a Wimpy Kid*, and the Nancy Drew series, all have these qualities. (See the Appendix, Handout 1, for a guide to choosing books to read aloud.)

Reflective Literacy in Context

Consider the many ways that the COVID-19 pandemic has affected the everyday lives of schoolchildren. They have lost daily, in-person contact with teachers and peers. They have lost the freedom to go to the playground, play sports, have their ballet classes, see movies, and visit neighbors. They are in the company of family members who may be highly anxious about the virus threat, have medical issues that make them vulnerable, are protecting elderly parents, or are sick with the virus themselves. They may have lost family members, without the benefit of in-person rituals of comfort and connection. Given the huge range of socioeconomic circumstances that in part determine the options for weeks and weeks of out-of-school time during the period of school closure, there will be children who stayed inside tiny apartments as well as children whose families have retreated to country houses or other safe havens. As teachers interface with children online, making literacy choices for read-alouds that reflect aspects of our collective experience can work to diminish the isolation that many children are feeling.

Think about the examples of the children during this time of disruption and loss addressed with reflective language earlier in the chapter. Since teachers often use multiple avenues to address issues in the classroom, use of the reflective literacy process with these same children will be explored below.

Elias. Elias is one of five children in his prekindergarten class who have late December birthdays and haven't yet turned 4. He and three of the other youngest children in the group indeed act developmentally younger than most of their peers, specifically when it comes to separation and object-constancy issues. These separation issues manifest during arrival, departure, transition in and out of the classroom for specials, lunch, and other occasions, and at playground time and during rest time. In addition to the presence of these very young children in the group, there were a few children in foster care who had traumatic separations from parents, as well as a few children who had experienced loss of a parent, grandparent, or sibling.

Following the protocol for reflective literacy, Elias's teacher Donna looked for "common ground issues" among the children in her classroom before making her book choices for her daily read-alouds. She had already done Story Gathering with a member of the children's families, so she thought about what she had come to know about her students *in* the classroom as well as in their lives *outside* of the classroom. Donna chooses the book *Wemberly Worried* (Henkes, 2000) to read to her group at storytime. In this story, the main character is a mouse named Wemberly who has many worries about starting school. Wemberly's worries included some of what her younger children and her children who have had many disruptions worried about. As Donna reads, she notices the children becoming increasingly engaged by the story and is particularly impressed by her group of "littlest" children, who are not poking, squirming, or popping up, but sitting or sprawling motionless on the carpet, focused on the illustrations as Donna reads the words. Some of the children with early losses or disrupted attachments are looking a little concerned or fragile as the story unfolds and seem relieved by the ending.

When the book is finished, Donna asks the children what they think about the story and what the story reminds them of. Several children raise their hands to respond.

Elias: It reminds me that before I came to kindergarten I was
   worried that the kids might hit me.
Donna: That must have made you want to stay home! (Elias nods.)
Kara: It reminds me of the day that my grandma [her foster mother]
   opened the cupboard, and a mouse was in there! Then she
   closed the cupboard fast, and it went away, and we didn't ever
   see it come back.
Donna: Does it remind you of that because Wemberly is a mouse?
Kara (nods): And I didn't want my grandmama to kill the mouse
   with a mouse trap because it might have been a nice mouse like
   Wemberly.

(Several other children contribute stories about mice at home.)

Donna: Wemberly has lots of worries in this story. Her worries are
   about starting school. Elias remembered a worry that he had
   before he started pre-K. Maybe other kids remember worries that
   they had before they came to school, or maybe, even new worries
   that came from being *in* school. (Several hands went up.)
Kimberly: Sometimes I was worried that no one was going to be my
   friend.
Jake: Once, no one came to pick me up from after school, and I was
   worried.
Jean Pierre: I was worried that when the lights went off at quiet time,
   then scary things might happen!
Kara: I was worried that when we went to the store to buy the
   pumpkin for Halloween, maybe my grandma might come to get
   me and she wouldn't be able to find me!

Donna used reflective language to acknowledge each child's comment. She then invited them to draw, and dictate or write their thoughts and feelings that came from the story. She assembled a new book comprised of each child's response. Elias's page had a tiny figure in a circle in the middle of the page, surrounded by big scary-looking faces. There was a little house in one corner and a bigger building in the other. He dictated, "This is the little puppy. He can bite all the big doggies on the way to school and do a scary growl! Grrrr!" Elias's drawing and dictation's theme of feeling small and vulnerable but finding a powerful fantasy to identify with came up in some of the other pages of this classroom book as well, giving Donna direction in her ongoing reflective literacy dialogue with the children in her group. She decided to read the story *Where the Wild Things Are* for the next read-aloud and added the books *The Little Engine That Could* and *Little Tug* to the book corner.

Luis and Fernando. Anya thought about Luis and Fernando and the many other undocumented and refuge children in her classroom and chose the book *Mis Zappatos Y Yo* (Laínez, 2019), which included bilingual text in both English and Spanish. Since Anya wasn't fluent in Spanish, she wanted something that the Spanish-dominant kids could review on their own after the read-aloud, to make sure that they didn't miss anything that might be meaningful to them. The book featured a boy called Tito, whose mother bought him new shoes before going to join her sister in America. The boy and his father were planning to join her eventually, but when life became too dangerous in their village, they had to begin the long journey on foot, over hills and through marshes and across two heavily guarded borders. By the time the boy and his father managed to reach the United States and were freed to join his mother and aunt, the worn-out shoes told the story of their long and difficult journey. As Anya read the story, the group was so silent that she could have heard a pin drop.

When Anya finished the story, the hush was broken by Miguel who said that when he came to America, his shoes were so torn that they had fallen off.

> *Miguel:* My uncle had to wrap up my feet with shirts! (He pointed to his feet. Some kids giggled. Others waved their hands to contribute to the dialogue.)
>
> *Cherllynn:* When my great grandpa moved up north from Alabama, he said he came with only the clothes on his back!

Annika: He must have gotten seriously tired of those clothes! (The girls giggled.)

Anya: Sometimes it's hard to imagine how much people have struggled just to get to our city! Some of you know from your own difficult journeys, and some have heard stories from your relatives. Now try to imagine what it was like for Tito to come to *school* in the United States after his difficult journey. How do you think he felt in the beginning? What do you think was scary for him? What do you think might have helped him? Use your journals to write a story about Tito at school, using those questions to guide your thinking. If you would like to share your story with everyone else, put your journal in this top basket when you're done. If you want me to be your only reader, put your journal in this bottom basket.

(The children scattered to their cubbies to retrieve their journals and began to write.)

Layla and Kaitlyn. As part of her action plan, the principal Heather encouraged Rosalyn, the 5th-grade teacher, to use reflective literacy as a way of addressing the complex social dynamics in her classroom. Rosalyn chose the chapter book *Awkward* by Svetlana Chemakova (2015) and read a chapter a day to the group for a few days before lunch until the book was finished. The story follows a girl through her first day of middle school, where she encounters kids who make her feel invisible or scared, finally by the end, finding one place in the new school where she feels safe and comfortable. Rosalyn made a conscious choice to use a book focusing on the dynamics of *middle school*, since concerns about the transition to middle school were frequently on the minds of 5th-graders and therefore might create a more receptive state to a story about peer dynamics. The themes were close enough to reflect the issues that were visceral in Rosalyn's classroom, but distant enough to provide a "cover" for the girls who motivated the teacher's story choice.

When the story was finished, Rosalyn had the kids sit in a circle on the carpet. She wondered aloud what the story made them think about. "Middle school!" the children answered in unison.

Rosalyn: I know middle school is on your mind these days. The story made me wonder how the main character had fit into the group when she was in elementary school. Do you think she had a lot of friends? Do you think she hung out with the popular kids? Do you think she felt safe?

Layla: I think she had a best friend in elementary school, but her best friend moved away before middle school started.

Daniel: I think she was a nerd in elementary school and is still a nerd in middle school! (Kids laugh, some retorting that "it takes one to know one." Daniel responds shrugging in a lighthearted way.) You should know!

Renata: I think she had friends in elementary school, but not the popular kids. But now that she found a safe group in middle school, she can decide if she wants to reinvent herself or not. My cousin said you can reinvent yourself in middle school!

Rosalyn: What does it mean to "reinvent yourself"?

Renata: It means you dress differently and act differently so different kids will like you, and you can be popular!

Rosalyn: How do the popular kids get to be popular? Is it always about reinventing?

(Kids call out responses, indicating mixed opinions.)

Cora: The popular kids are not always the nicest kids. That's why that girl in the story did not fit in with them, because she was too nice. The problem is that if you're too nice, kids think you're a nerd.

Daniel: So? At least you get to be yourself, and you can be funny!

Rosalyn: We'll continue this conversation on Friday. Meanwhile, before Friday, look at the questions on the board that relate to *Awkward.* Choose two of the questions and write a paragraph to respond to each.

Questions

1. If you were to reinvent yourself, who would you become? Why? How would you accomplish this? How do you think it would feel to become this new version of you?
2. Have you ever been left out of a group you wished you could be part of? What prevented you from being a part of that group? How did it feel to always be on the outside of somewhere you wanted to be? What advice would you give a 4th-grader about that situation?
3. Do popular kids have too much power? Why or why not? How do they get to be so powerful in a classroom or group?

4. Who did you identify with in the story of *Awkward*? Describe the ways in which you identified with him or her. Where do you imagine *your* safe place will be in middle school?

Analysis of the Reflective Literacy Process

Each of the teachers featured in these vignettes made literacy choices that reflected elements of developmental issues and life experiences that were familiar to the children in the group and influenced dynamics at school. The stories chosen invited exploration of these familiar themes, without didactic resolutions. In each instance, the teacher is learning what each child found meaningful about the story and how the story relates to that child's own experiences. In many instances, there is verbal and visual sharing, so that children can hear, see, and connect to peer-generated thoughts and feelings. This part of the process acts to decrease emotional and social isolation within the group, promoting resilience and diminishing risk for mental health issues as children move toward adolescence (National Academies of Sciences, Engineering, and Medicine, 2020).

Finally, Reflective Literacy gives children the gift of using literacy as a voice for their own thoughts, feelings, and life experiences, as well as connecting with the feelings of the other children they spend hours with each day. Through dictating, writing, and illustrating their own stories in response to what has been read, children generate stories with personal meaning and have the opportunity to hear and connect with what is meaningful to others. In the case of Elias, he was able to make a strong connection to a classmate whose story revealed an interest in tiny animals, leading to play where Elias and his classmates became superheroes who protect all animals in danger. In the case of Luis and Fernando, the story of *Mis Zappatos Y Yo* brought out several immigration stories among classmates that neither had been aware of prior. They were then able to broaden their circle of peers they felt safe and comfortable with in the classroom. In the case of Layla and Kaitlyn, each used their writing assignments to explore reinventing themselves, with Layla expressing her wish to become a leader instead of a follower, and Kaitlyn writing about her fantasy of attending middle school as an invisible superhero, who could spy on everyone and only become visible when she swooped in to save the day. (See the Appendix, Handout 2, Guide to Inviting Reflective Literacy Follow-Up Activities.)

Over time, their teacher Rosalyn noticed a subtle but real shift in the power dynamics in the room, as the girls who wrote about the power that the popular girls had came to realize they themselves could be powerful in ways they hadn't thought about before.

Reflective literacy is an iterative process that invites and follows the themes that emerge in the reflective language dialogue. Although this section focuses on developing a read-aloud dialogue between teacher and children, there are other creative literacy approaches that include reflective literacy components. See, for example, Vivian Paley's story-acting technique elaborated in Chapter 5 (Paley, 1991). Another reflective approach focuses on using teacher-made books that are tailor-made to reflect very specific issues or circumstances occurring in the lives of one or more children and explored in private or small group meetings. Still other ways of using reflective literacy within curriculum involve interpreting developmentally salient children's literature themes creatively through dance, visual art, or song (Mardell et al., 2013). Both reflective language and reflective literacy have the capacity to transform classroom climate, as children come to see themselves more and more consistently through a good mirror that portrays them as valued and worthy community members.

CHAPTER 5

Inviting and Containing the Voices of Children in School

Emotionally Responsive Practice (ERP) schools value a balanced classroom environment as a protective factor for child mental health and empowered learning. In order to create a balanced environment, teachers consider the existing classroom routines, practices, rules, and expressive outlets that run through the school day. We know that children need a predictable classroom routine and structure to feel secure and comfortable at school, but if this structure prohibits movement, self-expression, and social connection, it is unlikely to be sustainable for many children. Without invitations for self-expression woven through the school day, children who cannot "hold" the sadness, anxiety, anger, grief, trauma, and fear that they carry will likely explode before the day is over, creating disruption and chaos, and encountering angry, frustrated responses from teachers and school leaders. Without invitations for self-expression, children who can't hold emotional pain without exploding can be weighed down by what they carry, building risk for social and emotional isolation as they grow.

On the other hand, if a classroom environment is completely open-ended, without routine or limits clearly defined, and has only expressive outlets as organizing activities, things tend to become chaotic, overwhelming, and overstimulating for many children. Without containing routines or structures that can hold the continuum of feelings that children carry, children can become anxious and feel unsafe. Therefore, ERP involves creating classrooms with a balance of invitations for self-expression within containing routines and structures throughout the school day. (See the Appendix, Handout 3.)

A common routine in early childhood classrooms is morning meeting. Morning meeting happens at the same time each day, allowing children to predict the sequence of events, feel part of the group, and perhaps become oriented to the events that follow. Often, there are rituals involving the weather, the calendar, or greetings, which may also be predictable, reassuring, and affirming. Given the value of this containing routine, and the capacity of this routine to "hold" invitations, ERP class-room meetings would include one or more invitations for self-expression, and make room for those invitations by omitting a ritual that doesn't seem developmentally meaningful. The continuum of invitations might range from allowing children to create some new words to a familiar song to express feelings, thoughts, or ideas; using an interactive feelings chart before or during the meeting (see the Appendix, Handout 4); or imple-menting "News of the Day," which involves inviting children to share stories about anything new in their lives through dictation or writing prior to meeting, and then verbal story sharing as part of meeting time.

Similarly, many middle school programs include group advisory pe-riods during the school week. Advisory happens on a predictable sched-ule with the same teacher-advisor and group of designated children. Therefore, it can become a predictable, welcome downtime in the minds of young teens, and a time to inform students of upcoming events and requirements for teacher-advisors. However, ERP advisories also include *at least* one expressive invitation within the predictable structure of the advisory period, to allow the pause in an otherwise busy day to enhance community, connection to self and others, and the capacity to create and use metaphor in communication. An ERP advisory session might include a continuum of invitations, from writing two words on an index card that sums up each student's high and low points of the school day so far, to inviting students to draw their vision of a fantasy "safe space" at school, to allowing kids to talk freely within the community.

Contrary to the highly structured classroom environment often rec-ommended for children with social and emotional issues, a classroom with a balance of inviting and containing routines is able to give both *pos-itive and negative thoughts and feelings* a "place to live" at school, which can help to prevent emotional explosions. This creates a more sustainable learning environment for children who fight intrusive thoughts or power-ful memories that don't fit into scripted curriculum. When emergent themes can be folded into existing curricular structure in creative and fluid ways, children's investment in learning is heightened, and internal distraction is minimized.

EMERGENT CURRICULUM: LITERACY, SOCIAL STUDIES, AND ART

Teachers who have worked with the same age group for several years can identify developmental themes that emerge year after year after year. Teachers who have worked in a school or neighborhood for more than a few years can identify "common ground" experiences that come up in children's conversation, play, artwork, and writing. Inviting children to explore these themes on a deeper level within curriculum can be extremely valuable, heightening attention and motivation, diminishing social and emotional isolation, and helping children to integrate difficult experiences. In ERP, literacy, social studies, and art are the areas most easily informed by emergent themes. Since literacy examples were included in the prior chapter, examples of ERP-informed social studies and art will be included here.

Social Studies and Art: The Study of Ourselves in Context

Social studies lends itself to developmentally informed curriculum, often beginning with the study of family, school community, and neighborhood in the younger grades, and expanding to studies of history, geography, and culture in the upper grades. Active learning dovetails with social studies well, as children learn to grasp and expand abstract concepts through fieldtrips, first in their own neighborhoods and later expanding to places nearby and, as well as to past cultures accessed through museums and virtual means. Constructing their own version of these concepts allow children to make a deep connection to their studies in meaningful ways. Classrooms that follow fieldtrips with invitations to create the worlds being explored in miniature give children a sense of agency and empowerment.

For example, Crystal's 2nd-grade classroom studying the history of their own Brooklyn neighborhood takes a walk over the Brooklyn Bridge. They return to the classroom to discuss their observations and learning before beginning a project involving constructing a New York City bridge and the islands that it connects. In classroom community projects such as this, individual children have an invitation to portray their neighborhood and the surrounding communities as they see and understand them. Integrating the arts into this social studies curriculum allows children to use a variety of media to portray complex constructs that they may not initially be able to articulate. In addition, the co-constructing of "mini worlds" gives children experience with contributing to something larger than would be possible on their own, expanding their ability to compromise and regulate with a group.

Diego, an 8-year-old who entered Chrystal's class in the middle of the year, had lived in several foster homes before joining this classroom community. He often seemed distracted and perhaps felt at a loss to master curriculum that was different from the focus in his prior schools.

The 2nd-grade bridge project was engaging to Diego, much to Chrystal's relief. During a class discussion, Diego proudly shared that he had lived in every borough that the bridges they were learning about connected to. The other children were impressed, as some of them hadn't yet visited every borough. In this way, Diego's fund of knowledge became valued by his peers.

Once Upon a Time: Inviting Metaphor into the Healing Classroom

Creating symbol and metaphor in play, artwork, and story gives children a therapeutic avenue to integrate both emotional and cognitive learning. While the Common Core emphasizes informational texts, fictional texts can be thought provoking and conceptually rich. This is particularly true for young children and young adolescents, who have both reality and fantasy factors informing their thought processes. Creating symbol and metaphor can provide an important inner space for containing/holding overwhelming emotional experience. Resourceful teachers can find ways to embed creative processes within Common Core frameworks (see Figure 5.1).

Group creation of symbols and metaphor allow children to connect with one another around their cocreations, which may hold different emotional meaning for each child involved, but tap into common underlying issues. Inviting group cocreation of symbol and metaphor through original song lyrics, drama, murals, and so on, can give complex emotions a place to live outside of the brain and body, helping children to feel less burdened, and creating a stronger classroom community.

An example of a blended expressive arts/social studies curriculum may include Vivian Paley's (1991) story-acting technique, inviting children to dictate, write, and illustrate stories that subsequently can be dramatized by peer actors. When children in the early grades are encouraged to use the prompt "Once Upon a Time . . . ," their stories often include a blend of developmental and life experiences in the metaphor of "long ago." For example, during the bridge study, Diego's end-of-unit "Once Upon a Time" story might include the following narrative:

> Once upon a time there was a boy who sailed the sea and explored every island in the world. He was looking for an island that grew mangos, which he loved to eat. But none of the islands grew them, so he threw a mango pit on the ground and waited for it to rain. The End.

According to story-acting protocol, Diego would then choose peers to become the boy, the islands, the sailboat, and the rain, bringing his story to life. Diego would act as the director of the mini-production.

Figure 5.1. Responsive Themes Within Common Core Framework

Common Core Standards	Addressing "Core" Issues	Study Topics	Learning Opportunity
KSL1: Participate in collaborative conversations with diverse peers and adults in small and large groups and during play.	Friendship and Belonging	Friends and Neighbors	Peer interviews re: history of friendships. (How friends met and what made them become friends.)
			What are neighbors? How do neighbors contribute to make a neighborhood? Teddy Bear Neighborhood Project.
	Identity	Who Am I? Who Are You?	Can friends have different likes and dislikes and still be friends?
		Same and Different.	Charts and easel.
		Connections	Can children have more than one friend at a time? Charts and easel.
KW2: Use a combination of drawing, dictating, oral expression, and/or emergent writing to name a familiar topic and supply information	Power and Powerlessness	Powerful Community Figures	Who are the powerful people at school? How did they become powerful? Research Project.
		Power of Wishes	Who are the powerful people in the neighborhood? How did they become powerful? Research Project.
		Superheroes: Real and Pretend	What is the difference between real and pretend superheroes?
KW4: Create a response to a text, author, or personal experience (e.g., dramatization, artwork, or poem).			Magic-wand activity: A wish for your own superpower.
			A plan for your own superpower.

ERP teachers can see evidence of Diego's social studies curriculum learning in his story, as well as his ability to create a metaphor for his *own* life story as a foster child. They appreciate the social–emotional value of Diego's creation. His ability to respond to his teacher Crystal's invitation to invent a story and to use the classroom model of drama to "give his story a place to live" speaks to Diego's potential to use academic tools to integrate difficult life experiences. The story ends hopefully, which might reflect the "good mirror" that Diego gets from his teacher every day. Although Diego was vulnerable to acting out during his first weeks in the classroom, using symbol and metaphor to create and hold emotional content seemed to diminish his need to enact his history in disruptive ways.

"GHOST-BUSTING" IN SHARED SPACES

Shared spaces and shared routines can become "haunted" in schools. Generally speaking, shared spaces and shared routines are managed by only a few adults who are monitoring large groups of children whom they do not know well. This can create a dynamic where children feel uncontained and unsafe, and act in ways that challenge the staff's capacity to cope. In addition, shared spaces and shared routines such as lunch in the cafeteria, free time on the playground, or traveling in the hallways can involve making transitions away from core teachers, often leaving children vulnerable to feelings of loss, and subsequent loss of emotional equilibrium. The noise and high-energy levels that result can be overwhelming and overstimulating, even to those children who are creating the havoc.

Cafeteria

The cafeteria is especially susceptible to "ghost hosting," as caregiving routines of eating (and rest for younger students) can trigger feelings of conflict or abandonment for children. In school cafeterias, the routine of mealtime, often associated with the intimate environment of home, takes place in a very large, impersonal space. There are frequently few adults, and those that are in place may not have strong relationships with the children. Therefore, the cafeteria can bring up a yearning for parents, as well as times when adults were demanding or anxious around children's eating habits, or times when children were worried about having enough food. The cafeteria sometimes feels chaotic and out of control, leading to children acting in unsafe ways.

Principals who infuse shared routines and shared spaces with inviting and containing strategies and structures may organize daily routines in intentional ways, enhancing adult–child connection and diminishing reactivity in children and in monitoring adults. For example, during lunchtime, ERP principals may implement one or several of the following preventive strategies to create a more emotionally supportive environment:

Supporting the Holding Power of Space

- *Children are seated at round tables* to invite conversation and connection and contain energy.
- *Laminated* (or otherwise enclosed) *artworks* from each classroom/grade level are posted to affirm value of self-expression in student work.
- *Soft classical music is playing in the background* to promote a calm and containing atmosphere.
- *Designated tables* for pre-K and kindergarten children provide predictable, containing, familiar experience.
- *Outdoor spaces have designated activity areas and age level materials* to invite specific interactive activities within a contained area (i.e., climbing area for pre-K and kindergarten; open area for use of colored chalk, jump ropes, large rubber balls, and so on, for lower grades; basketball nets and balls, mural spaces for upper grades).

Enhancing Large Group Routines

- *Kindergarten and 5th-grade "Reading and Eating Buddies"* programs partner 5th-graders and kindergarten buddies at lunchtime, inviting connection and containing 5th-grade energy in productive ways.
- Small group *lunches with principal/AP/guidance counselor* invite conversation and feedback about school routines and contain diffuse energy.
- *Placemats project for kindergarten lunch* (i.e., designing, creating, and using laminated placemats made in the classroom) maintains connection with classroom teacher and contains space through feelings of ownership.
- *After-lunch interest groups* (e.g., Art group, Improve Our School group, Movie Watchers/Reviewers group) provide activities that are engaging to children and offer social connection within more manageable and more intimate, containing structures.

Rather than prohibit interaction between children in the cafeteria, or assume that complete chaos is inevitable, Emotionally Responsive principals work to provide a middle ground involving a better balance of inviting activities and containing spaces and structures. These interventions help to banish the "ghosts" that invade shared spaces and shared routines in schools, during the times when children are without their primary school attachment partners.

Library

The school library can be a place of engagement and respite in Emotionally Responsive schools. By nature, the library is a resource for schoolchildren. They are often read to in groups during library time when they are little and can then choose books to take home with them, creating a bridge between home and school. As they go through the grades, children can gradually learn to use the library to follow their individual interests through literacy. Early experiences in the library can set the stage for intentional use of the library as a space of respite, calm, and contained activity, especially if there are a variety of resources that provide a "good mirror" for children, no matter what their academic level or emotional state. In order for the library to become a centering space, the librarian must be in sync with the mission of making the library an Emotionally Responsive environment. Although it may be difficult for a librarian to get to know every child, since typically all of the children in school use the library each week or month, the librarian may be one of the few adults in the building to observe the children as they grow through the grades. Therefore, working in concert with teachers and school mental health staff, the librarian can become an important resource in containing children in need, and inviting them to pursue their interests and talents.

TOO MUCH, NOT ENOUGH, JUST RIGHT

The balance of inviting and containing components may vary from classroom to classroom, depending on the needs of the children, the time of the school year, and other factors. Many schools focus on introducing containing factors in the beginning of the year, emphasizing routines and rituals to help children settle in. Once routines and rituals are in place (or sometimes even before), public school teachers are encouraged to dive into academics before they know how to make the learning meaning-ful to the children in front of them, circumventing a critical pathway to learning. Many teachers are forced to race the clock so that they will have enough time to cover the prescribed material, eliminating any downtime, or time to connect with individual children beyond assessing their skills, or time to help children to connect to one another in supportive, genuine ways.

When schools follow a "Containing Only" path, children may feel temporarily less anxious and more organized but are essentially left alone to make sense of complex social dynamics and personal feelings at school. Schoolwork can seem like a distraction from those more pressing issues. Those children who don't seem to internalize rules and routines even though they can recite classroom and school rules by heart become obsta-cles to what the school may consider to be successful outcomes—staying "on track" and "on time."

Schools that use ERP guide their balance of inviting and containing using developmental factors as well as life experience factors to cre-ate a "just right" balance for their particular group of children. For example, a group with more than a few extremely active children may need group meetings to be shorter, but may need them to happen more than once a day. Children who have trouble regulating may need an inviting strategy sandwiched in between two containing structures. A classroom full of highly focused, upper-grade children who are per-fectionists, competitive with one another and highly stressed, may be academically in sync, but building emotional risk without intermittent invitations for connection and self-reflection. Unlike traditional ap-proaches that use standardized testing outcomes to measure a teacher's success, the ERP approach uses evidence of child well-being and focuses on whether children are demonstrating that the learning is meaningful to them. This way of working is compatible with authentic assessment, or performance-based assessment, recommended by the New York Per-formance Standards Consortium, advocated by well-known educators and advocates, Deborah Meier (Knoester & Meier, 2017) and Diane Ravitch (2020).

INVITING AND CONTAINING IN WORK WITH FAMILIES

Although many independent schools welcome lower-grade parents to bring their children into the school building and accompany them to the classroom each morning, urban public schools rarely extend this invitation. Typically, children and parents in public schools must separate in the school yard from kindergarten onward. Some schools even require this of pre-K children and their parents. There is often a strong feeling that the school's approach to parents must be all containing in order for schools to run smoothly. Invitations for parent participation are frequently limited to PTA, parent conferences, and end-of-year celebrations.

An all-containing approach to parents does make life in schools less complicated in some ways, but gives children and parents very mixed messages about their worth. Parents are ONLY welcome if they are able to contribute to the school's mission on a regular schedule. Typically, parents who are able to do that have more resources than other parents might, and children become aware of where their own parents fall on the continuum of "asset versus burden" as they grow into the upper elementary grades.

Often, parents who have the most difficulty establishing positive relationships at school are parents whose own school experiences were difficult. With no invitations to take in their child's school culture, classroom practice, and curriculum, such parents are left only with their own negative memories of school life to project into the building that keeps them out. This approach can result in parental outbursts at the security guard's desk, complaints to the superintendent, and a gulf between parents' projections and children's actual experiences that children may be unable to bridge.

Educators in ERP schools think about ways to balance containing structures with invitations for parent participation that are meaningful and inclusive. These invitations frequently include some in-classroom processes (publication celebrations, art shows, social studies museums, etc.) and occasional evening or weekend special events, such as movie nights, quilt making, as well as parent engagement groups.

Invitations to parents and families at ERP-informed schools routinely include both *Story-Gathering* and *parent engagement groups*. As introduced in Chapter 3, Story Gathering involves teachers meeting with parents or other family members to learn the important stories of each of their children's lives, allowing teachers to better understand and support social and emotional growth within the context of the child's actual experiences (Koplow, 2002). These conferences allow parents to experience the teacher's capacity to listen in a nonjudgmental way. ERP parent engagement groups invite parents to share their own experiences as schoolchildren with one another, and to explore the similarities and differences in those times verses their own children's experiences in school in the here and now. Parent engagement group facilitators use expressive arts modalities to encourage self-expression through symbol and metaphor, while circumventing language barriers that may exist (see Figure 5.2). Parent engagement groups work to diminish emotional and social isolation in the parent community and give parents a hands-on experience with active, expressive arts-based literacy and learning.

Finally, schools that offer families a balance of invitations for participation within containing activities and structures give them new imagery for school life, allowing present experiences to counter or provide balance to negative imagery that may linger from the past. When there is a

Figure 5.2. Story Quilt: Parent Engagement Project

"My quilt square tells a story. The circles are for my family members. The empty space is for when I lost my sister. The third circle is for when we adopted her daughter." (A parent group participant)

parallel level of commitment to children and their families, schools increase their potential to become communities where children thrive, and teachers gain an essential knowledge base for supporting the children they teach.

CHAPTER 6

Feeling Safe Changes Everything

ERP as Trauma-Informed Care

When children's experiences have been traumatic, their traumatic history comes to school with them. It may be present in their affects, in their approach to people in authority, in their expectations of harm when interacting with other children or adults, and in their hyperreactivity or withdrawal responses to perceived threats. Children with a traumatic history often feel unsafe at school and act in ways that make teachers and other children feel unsafe as well. In addition, trauma may present insidious effects on learning, interfering with what children are able to take in, think about, and retain (Pechtel & Pizzagalli, 2011; Terr, 1992; Terr et al., 1999).

Given the high incidence of trauma in the community of children residing in the United States, there has been an increasing focus on trauma education for teachers and school leaders. In order for trauma education to result in trauma-informed care in the school setting, multiple multifaceted relationship issues and systems issues must be addressed to meet the needs of both the children and the staff within that school community. In other words, in order for teachers and school leaders to help children feel safe at school, the policies and procedures of both instructional and noninstructional time must be supportive to both children and adults in the building. Teachers must feel safe themselves if children are to feel safe. Whether teachers and children feel endangered by the physicality of out-of-control students or by the state's threat of closure if test scores don't rise, trying to function with high levels of stress and anxiety in school can diminish efficacy for both traumatized adults and children. This is especially true in the context of the *community trauma*, currently brought to bear by COVID-19 and the escalation of racially motivated police brutality.

In the past, community trauma such as 9/11, Hurricane Katrina, and Hurricane Sandy frequently brought trauma awareness into schools, but often consisted of trauma recognition and referral, without informing classroom and school practice with a knowledge base that can prevent retraumatization.

Conversely, making schools become safe, low-stress environments allows both children and adults to weave a safety net that can be strong enough to hold traumatic history and buffer some of its most toxic secondary effects on socialization and learning. Emotionally Responsive Practice (ERP) offers a blueprint for the development of an infrastructure to support a relationship-based, trauma-informed care model that dovetails with the U.S. Substance Abuse and Mental Health Services Administration's 4 Rs for trauma-sensitive practice. These include:

1. Realizing the widespread impact of trauma.
2. Recognizing the signs of trauma.
3. Responding by fully integrating knowledge about trauma into policies, procedures, and practices.
4. Resisting the retraumatization of children and the adults who care for them (SAMHSA, 2014).

TRAUMA COMES TO SCHOOL

Understanding trauma both in clinical and biological terms can help teachers and school leaders to recognize its "voice" in the classroom, cafeteria, or administrative office. Once considered a low-incidence occurrence in the lives of American children, recent studies on the prevalence of childhood trauma reveal rates of 40%–60% of children experiencing at least one single incident trauma before the age of 8, with 60%–90% of young black and Hispanic children living in high poverty states experiencing multiple traumas (Sacks & Murphy, 2018.) Indeed, at the present time, pandemic statistics reveal striking disparities, with rates of illness and death among people of color three times as high as those affecting white people, leaving children of color more vulnerable to experiencing primary traumatic loss. It is not difficult to see how systemic inequities underly the discrepancy in exposure to traumatic experience.

Trauma's voice may come from one or several children within the school community, or may come from one or several adults within that community. The adult presentation may come from the school's parent community or the school's community of staff. Indeed, research finds that teachers and caregivers have a higher incidence of adverse childhood experiences than the population at large, and may have higher rates of traumatic history as well (Brickley & Guyton, 2015). In addition, vicarious trauma, or secondary trauma, affects a large number of classroom teachers, who spend many hours a day in the company of traumatized children (Borntrager et al., 2012). Secondary trauma, or the emotional experience of spending long periods of time taking in the traumatic affects, stories, and reenactments from children who are trauma affected, may contribute to high attrition rates among teachers. Recognizing the presentations of various types of traumatic experiences may help teachers feel more informed and perhaps less overwhelmed in the company of children who carry traumatic history.

Single-Incident Trauma

Trauma, by definition, is the result of an event or series of events that overwhelm the person's ability to cope physiologically, psychologically, emotionally, and spiritually (Substance Abuse and Mental Health Services Administration, 2012). Therefore, the experience of trauma and results of traumatic experience may vary from person to person. The context in which the trauma occurs is a relevant factor. For instance, if a single-incident trauma happens in a neutral context and is something that no one can anticipate, such as a house exploding suddenly because of a gas leak, a person who happens to be passing by this house as the event occurs is completely overwhelmed by the unanticipated, terrifying experience, on both a physiological level and the psychological level. Assuming the person was feeling relatively safe and relaxed before walking by, his, her, or their sense of well-being is suddenly shattered by the event, which can occupy the "front" of the mind like a slow-motion video for a long time, including the smells, sounds, and sights that accompanied the explosion (Terr, 1992; Van der Kolk, 2000). If the child or adult was on the way to school when this happened, this traumatic event would likely prevent the taking in of new learning or social nuances from peers that morning. The child would be unlikely to be able to attend to the here and now without a bridge to the traumatic experience (Terr, 1992).

Many factors determine how much time will ameliorate this trauma-preoccupied state, including prior strengths and vulnerabilities, history of prior trauma, and available relationship support. If no one else was present during this single incident, the traumatic experience can become emotionally isolating, sometimes leading to social isolation which exacerbates the threat that post-traumatic stress disorder will result in ongoing mental health and learning challenges (Cook et al., 2005).

Multi-Incident Trauma

Multi-incident trauma has a different path because it has happened before and is therefore both known and unknown by its victims. Multi-incident trauma includes physical, emotional, and sexual abuse, as well as domestic violence and repeated exposure to societal violence. When multi-incident societal trauma has been intergenerational, caused or ignored by the powers that be, as has been the case in African American history, Native American history, and the history of many immigrant populations, the expectation of protection is minimal, and traumatic stress often lives in the bodies of group members and their children whether or not they themselves have experienced the traumatic events (Coleman, 2016; Powers et al., 2020; Stevens, 2020).

Because multi-incident trauma can happen as part of a predictable sequence of events, victims who feel unable to physically escape the threat of traumatic injury, instead escape psychologically, by dissociating themselves from their traumatic experience while it is happening. The dissociation allows them to distance themselves from what is happening to them, causing holes in memory for the traumatic event, as well as for things that happen before and after it occurs (Hagan, Hulette, & Lieberman, 2015; Terr, 1992; Perry, 2000).

Multi-incident trauma victims may come to school in a vulnerable state, without being able to connect to what happened between one school day and the other, and without memory for the learning that occurred the day before. Traumatized children may remain vulnerable to environmental triggers that elicit traumatic affects, blur past and present, and motivate behavior that seems out of sync with what is occurring in the here and now, as the event causes the traumatic experience to break through.

Sometimes, triggers may result in a return to the dissociated state, where children seem disconnected from themselves and others, as well as disconnected from what is going on around them in the classroom. Not being available to be psychologically present or attentive in the classroom can elicit negative responses from teachers, compounding the effects of the traumatic experiences and interrupting the learning process (Wright, 2014).

Complex Trauma

Complex trauma is the result of severe or multiple single-incident or multi-incident traumas occurring when children are very young, within the intimate environment of early caregiving relationships. Because the very young child's developmental process is just beginning, the trauma can interfere with the essential foundational experiences that underlie resolution of social, emotional, and cognitive integration. As children's brains develop within an environment of relationships, *trauma that occurs within the relationship, or trauma that occurs within the intimate relationship environment and is not buffered by other strong relationships with attached adults,* can disrupt the flow of attachment-based interactions that feeds the infrastructure of the young child's developing brain (National Scientific Council on the Developing Child, 2005, 2010b, 2018; Perry, 2000).

Early complex trauma can fragment attachment and can compromise the development of trust in the environment, creating a complex and disorganizing ripple effect through brain, body, and spirit of the very young child at a critical period. Therefore, the effects of *unattended*, complex trauma can be enduring as children grow (Cook et al., 2005; Van der Kolk, 2003). An infant or young toddler suffering from ongoing multi-incident, complex trauma has not yet had the developmental readiness to accomplish basic developmental milestones essential for healthy social, emotional, and cognitive growth. These are dependent on safe and supportive attachment relationships in order to unfold little by little throughout toddlerhood. Since the effects of complex trauma are many and cross developmental lines, complex trauma syndrome has also been called *developmental trauma.*

Although unattended complex trauma can result in enduring developmental and psychological issues, *nurturing relationships with adults can buffer complex trauma and create a developmental foundation for growth and healing.* When a parent or family member can create a buffer for a child's traumatic experience, outcomes are more hopeful. When traumatic experience surrounds both the baby and the parent and undermines the parent's ability to buffer the trauma, very young children are often without the protective factors that create emotional balance. The overwhelming experiences can interfere with essential foundations for regulating emotion, mastering regulation of state, maintaining equilibrium during transitions, as well as undermining the development of the cognitive infrastructure for symbolic thought.

Timing is relevant to childhood presentation of traumatic history, in ways that may be counterintuitive. Many people assume that babies and toddlers are "too little" to be able to take in the traumatic event or events, or will "forget" what happened. In actuality, the youngest victims may be the most deeply affected, as they are unable to understand what is happening to them, but take in the traumatic affects, emotional pain, and overwhelming sensory intrusions on psychological and physiological levels nonetheless (Lieberman et al., 2011; Perry, 2000; Van der Kolk, 2015). Even though the trauma may not be available to conscious memory, it lives in the body and may later surface in behavior, dreams, and dramatic play as children grow (Cook et al., 2005; Terr, 1992).

When very young children are developing in an environment that threatens their well-being, their brains produce high levels of adrenaline and cortisol, to enable survival reactivity (fight or flight), simultaneously shutting down neuron production and the creation of new connective synopsis while in reactive states (Hertzman & Boyce, 2010; National Scientific Council on the Developing Child, 2010b). Because trauma can derail the developmental process of babies, toddlers, and very young children, it often produces a complex picture that is distinctive from the traumatic reactions of teen or adult trauma survivors, whose developmental foundations are already in place. Therefore, *attending to* complex trauma in children and families becomes essential as young traumatized children grow and enter the world of early childhood and elementary school programs. The adults who will be part of children's day-to-day lives in school have the potential to use their relationships with children to *buffer* the effects of trauma, and to support children's social and emotional development and learning. Supporting families so that they are more able to buffer traumatic experiences for their children is paramount, while the resources to provide this support are missing from the national agenda.

RECOGNIZING AND RESPONDING TO TRAUMA'S VOICE

Traumatized children often behave in ways that confuse and frighten other children and adults in the school setting. For instance, a child with a story of multi-incident trauma beginning at age 4 may regress in many of the areas where there had been prior mastery, such as toileting and self-generated play, giving adults who know him pause to consider that the child's regressed behavior is experience related. If the traumatic experience is unremitting and without adult buffering, such as in many cases of domestic violence, for example, the energy needed to master 4-year-old milestones of investing in peer relationships, identity issues, and finding healthy ways to feel powerful may be surrendered, as the child struggles to cope with the traumatic experiences.

If the child is not well known by adults at school, or has been in multiple settings, there is a danger that adults may see him as slow, socially unpredictable, lacking attentional capacity or simply disinterested in peers or in the early childhood curriculum. A child who is not viewed through the lens of life experiences may receive inaccurate reflections from frustrated teachers, who may see him as intentionally unresponsive, difficult, or aggressive. If adults reflect that negative picture to the child, the inaccurate reflection becomes a "bad mirror" that can further distort self-image for a child who comes to school with traumatic history.

Because identity issues and issues of power and powerlessness are in play for 4-year-olds (see Figure 2.1 in Chapter 2), there is a secondary risk of the child becoming identified with the aggressor in the domestic violence arena. Children do this in order to avoid feeling powerless, often resulting in aggressive behavior toward more physically vulnerable children at school. As a child who identifies with the aggressor is likely to use "adult" language, affects and postures that were taken in during traumatic times, his threatening behavior is likely to illicit angry, defensive responses from both other children and adults in the classroom. When this happens, the traumatized 4-year-old in pain often becomes more and more invisible, and harder and harder to empathize with. Instead of providing a "good mirror" for the traumatized 4-year-old, adults and children may take in the aggressive adult persona as a threat to their own well-being and efficacy, convincing themselves and the child that he has become a dangerous element who must be expelled. Indeed, research shows that early childhood expulsion rates are significantly higher than K–12 expulsion rates, with boys of color being more likely than white boys to be expelled (Gilliam, 2005). Studies on the adverse experiences of expelled young children reveal a likely connection between traumatic history and school exclusion (Bartlett et al., 2017).

Older children with traumatic history may come to school with some or many early developmental milestones unresolved, leaving them at a loss during the transitions, routine separations, and the fast-moving curriculum demands that fill their school days. In score-driven school environments, the routines and behavior management styles employed not only fail to inhibit fight or flight responses for children with traumatic history, *but can actively trigger* those responses in predictable ways. For example, a child who lives with domestic violence where raised voices predict physical aggression is likely to become unglued or aggressive if the school security guard screams in his face because he is talking loudly as the class walks down the hall.

Figure 6.1 features several symptoms that children with traumatic history often show in the classroom. Staff may have seen and heard these behaviors and interactive patterns, but may not have recognized them

Figure 6.1. Recognizing and Responding to Trauma in Children

Trauma's "Voice"	Staff Response	Indications	ERP Follow Up
Traumatic Affects • Preoccupied, faraway look, or terrified expression • Aggressive affect that is unfamiliar, as though it is "borrowed" • Dissociated state where child appears disconnected from the here and now	• Gentle approach • Soft voice tone • Verbal reflection of observable status Ex.: "You look like you are far, far away in your mind"; "You look like something scary just happened"; etc.	• A traumatic experience is taking up the child's mental space. The child may be "lost" in a traumatic moment. • Something in the school environment may have triggered a feeling from a traumatic experience.	• Offer opportunity for the child to write or draw in a journal. • Invite the child to tell you about the trauma if they would like to. • Offer a seat close to a staff member to diminish isolation and enhance connection.
Hypervigilance and Hyperarousal	• Gentle approach • Reassuring voice tone • Articulate teacher's mission to keep children safe at school. • Interpret source of distracting elements. Ex.: "That was the sound of the radiator working hard to keep us warm."	The child has not been kept safe at some point in time and feels he must safeguard his own well-being by maintaining his attention on the externals of the room: door and windows.	Forecast changes with disruptions. (New adults in the room, fire drills, shelter-in-place drills, etc.) • Explain the source of unfamiliar noises. • Hold the child's hand on fieldtrips.
Hyperactivity and Hyperreactivity	• Build in time to move. Allow for various work positions. Verbally acknowledge that some children need to move while they are learning.	• The child may have high levels of stress hormones triggering responses to take action before being able to think things through.	• Orchestrate psychological home base. "Do your drawing, and then come and show me," etc.

94

	• Verbalize cause and effect re: activity level and hyperreactivity. Ex.: "Anna is upset because when you jump up, she can't see the picture I am showing." "Matthew bumped you by accident, but you thought it was on purpose and now both of you are upset!"	• The child may not have achieved the milestone of psychological home base, and therefore may not know how to use the teacher as a way of orienting in the classroom. • The child may be unable to tolerate inactive periods. Rest times or unoccupied waiting may increase vulnerability to emotional flooding.	• Arrange the room with clear definition and purpose of the various materials and spaces included. • Avoid open room with all furniture on the perimeter.
Traumatic Play Play that is grim, repetitive themed, or play that incorporates affects of a traumatic experience, i.e., high-pitched, alarming screaming during firefighter play, hyperventilating after reciting dramatic lines in a school play.	In a calm, supportive manner, the teacher can reflect on what he or she sees and hears, helping child differentiate past and present. Ex.: "You and Monica were playing about firefighters, but your voice sounds like someone who is REALLY in a fire! Maybe you remember a time when there WAS a fire! Right now, there's no smoke and no flames, only make believe."	The child is using play to try to master events that left him or her traumatized, but is getting stuck because the play becomes retraumatizing. The child requires play therapy in order to gain mastery of the traumatic event in context of a therapeutic relationship with an adult.	The teacher can make note of the themes that become traumatic during play. The teacher can refer the child to school social worker or school psychologist for additional support.

(*continued*)

95

Figure 6.1. (continued)

Trauma's "Voice"	Staff Response	Indications	ERP Follow Up
Flashbacks Reexperiencing a traumatic experience that happened in the past as though it were happening in the present, usually triggered by a sound, sight, or smell in the present. Ex.: Police are passing by, an adult yelling, loud music, etc.	In a clear voice, use the phrase "Maybe you remember." Ex.: "Maybe you remember when something scary happened with the police, but now you're with our class and we are going to visit the library. See?" (Point to library.) If the flashback is happening in the classroom, bring the child with you to look in the mirror, where he or she can see that she is with you.	Something in the here and now triggered a traumatic memory from the past that feels like it is happening in the present. The child is unable to differentiate past from present in that moment.	Make a note of any environmental trigger that seems connected to the flashback. Support child ahead of time if the triggers are predictable. Ex.: "Sometimes when we go on trips and police cars go by, it gets really scary for you, so how about if you be my partner for the trip that's coming up?"
Panic Attacks Panic attacks in children may start out as tantrums, or resemble tantrums, but differ in important ways. Tantruming generally happens within a relationship. Tantruming children want to be in the presence of the adult they are protesting. However, during a panic attack, children seem to lose contact with the adult as the physiology of panic takes over. Typically, there are physical symptoms such as rapid heartbeat, sweating, trembling, vomiting, and wetting.	A child in the middle of a panic attack cannot usually take in what the adult is saying. The adult can focus on keeping the child safe and keeping other children at a safe distance. The adult can interpret the panic to the other children in a reassuring manner. Ex.: "Noah is so upset right now that he can't really stop and think, so we will wait until he feels calmer before we ask him to join us."	The child has become overwhelmed with traumatic emotions that cannot be verbalized or symbolized. Traumatic stress has become more than the child is able to manage. Children may eventually wear themselves out and fall asleep or may eventually begin to cry and seek comfort from the adult.	ERP teachers and school leaders know that panic is something that is happening to the child, not behavior that the child can inhibit or control. After a panic attack, the adult can express empathy for the child's level of distress, and offer to partner with child to recognize signals that he or she is becoming overwhelmed and needs to get some water, seek the cozy corner, etc.

96

as "trauma's voice." In order to respond to the voices of trauma constructively, the healing school can apply the ERP techniques explored in previous chapters to maintain an emotionally balanced classroom climate, including verbal reflection and mirroring with empathy, focus on social and emotional cause and effect, and verbal differentiating of past from present. Use of transitional objects can also be explored (Koplow, 2008).

Trauma, Distance, and Empathy

Traumatic affects can feel contagious in the classroom, especially when there are more than a few children present with traumatic history. Teachers and other children can feel overwhelmed when surrounded by the voices of trauma, especially if they themselves have had traumatic experiences. In order for teachers to maintain empathy for children with traumatic history who may act in demanding and disturbing ways, school leaders must have empathy for the work of teachers. When there is no empathy for the teachers who spend hours a day in the company of traumatized children, teachers may need to keep the children at a distance in order to survive classroom life, and may react to difficult behavior in punitive, intolerant ways. Sadly, demeaning responses put traumatized children at additional risk, confirming negative self-worth and foregoing the potential for positive relationship support, inherent in a nurturing teacher–child relationship.

Media, Development, and Virtual Trauma

Finally, it is important to consider the developmental dilemmas of the thousands of young children who are underprotected from the virtual world, spending hours every day watching violent, terrifying, or overwhelming images on phones and tablets. Depending on the age and developmental level of the children watching, they may be unable to differentiate fantasy from reality, especially if the fantasy is complete with realistic-looking images that make scary figures "come to life." Without an adult present who can buffer, interpret, or simply prevent access, children who are caught in the loop of media overexposure may show symptoms of "virtual trauma," including nightmares, distracted and preoccupied state, inattention, hypervigilance, hyperactivity, and counterphobic behavior, whether or not they have actually experienced traumatic events in their own lives.

When children are overwhelmed by confusing experience or exposure, they may be driven to reenact what they have taken in. Disturbing media themes may be repeated in play, acted out in behavior, and/or stimulate craving for additional exposure in an attempt to control or master what feels impossible to integrate. The paradoxical behavior of children in the grip of virtual trauma can be confusing to parents, who may interpret media-driven behavior as a sign of interest or comfort with the disturbing material. In reality, children who are in the grip of virtual trauma often seem vulnerable to counterphobic reactions, craving what is actually terrifying to them. Parent education can be instrumental for such children who are desperately in need of adult partnership to prevent traumatization, as well as school-based group process and curriculum that supports differentiation of the virtual world from the real world.

Community Trauma: Lessons from Hurricane Sandy and COVID-19

Community trauma, or a traumatic incident that affects everyone in a town, city, state, and so on, is more often caused by a natural disaster, act of terrorism, or, in the case of COVID-19, epidemic. Community trauma can be devastating, often causing destruction of housing and infrastructure and loss of life. A distinctive feature of community trauma is that it is widely acknowledged, while personal trauma is often hidden or denied. Although hidden trauma victims generally struggle alone, the fact that community trauma is acknowledged *has the potential* to bring multiple levels of support to its victims, although politics often impact *when* these supports become available and *who* receives them. Since emotional isolation is a secondary effect of personal trauma, those who live through community trauma generally feel more permission to reach out to others for comfort, or to provide comfort to others in distress.

COVID-19 brings a conflict to affected communities throughout the world, since the actions of quarantine and stay-at-home orders that are necessary for maintaining physical health increase social and emotional isolation and are antithetical to maintaining mental health within a context of trauma and loss. At the time of this writing, most U.S. schools are still closed, and struggling to figure out how to provide a safe environment for children and staff as the school year approaches. When the schools reopen, the impact of trauma, loss, and isolation will be present in many classrooms.

BUILDING INFRASTRUCTURE FOR TRAUMA-INFORMED CARE

Schools that adopt a healing mission know that the human brain remains a work in progress throughout adolescence and into adulthood, and that organizing the school environment in emotionally responsive ways can promote a physiological and psychological feeling of safety, allowing a more hopeful trajectory for emotional stability, social integrity, and access to cognition. ERP-informed schools know that not only is it necessary to provide guidance for *recognizing* the presentation of trauma in the educational setting, but it is also crucial to follow through on informing school policies and practices with this knowledge base on a day-to-day basis so that children feel safe and protected. For children with traumatic history, and for the adults that are caring for them in school, feeling safe changes everything.

There are many components of the school day that may be informed by our knowledge base about child development and traumatic experience. The first components to be considered are the school's *routines and transitions*. School leaders might look at existing routines that comprise the school day, as well as the transitions between those routines. Even though districts tend to emphasize the value of instructional time, attention to improving the emotional and social supports during *noninstructional time* creates a more sustainable context for learning to take place. For children with traumatic history, the emotional climate of the surround can determine their degree of access to cognitive abilities as well as heightening or diminishing vulnerability to social issues. Whether the school setting accommodates toddlers and preschool children, elementary school children or middle school children, routines for children with traumatic history need to include the following components:

1. Consistency and clarity
2. Stable staffing
3. Connection to known adults, especially during *caregiving routines*, such as lunch, which can evoke connections to a traumatic context
4. Comforting rituals, especially at arrival and departure
5. Acknowledgment of presence and absence, or of unavoidable changes
6. Gradual timeframes to avoid physical crowding
7. Large group gatherings made smaller
8. As few transitions as possible

Whether the school setting accommodates toddlers and preschool children, elementary schoolchildren, or middle schoolchildren, *transitions* for groups that include children with traumatic history need to include the following components:

1. Soothing sounds and sights
2. Adult supervision and partnering
3. Forecasting
4. Continuity of staffing
5. Connection to (availability of) classroom teacher, social worker, and school leaders during transition
6. Minimal unoccupied waiting
7. Buddy systems

Whether the school setting accommodates toddlers and preschool children, elementary schoolchildren, or middle schoolchildren, *physical space* for groups that include children with traumatic history need to include the following components:

1. Comforting objects, colors, and patterns
2. Small spaces embedded in larger ones (e.g., a cozy corner within the classroom)
3. Soft items, like pillows, rugs, and sofas
4. Round tables in eating spaces
5. Available and accessible food when needed
6. Available and accessible water when needed
7. Clean, well-lit, and well-cared-for bathrooms
8. Features that define area use (e.g., art supplies imply that the area is used to create art)
9. Cozy corners accessible for retreat and comfort when stressed
10. Children's work and photos well protected and displayed as valuable
11. Outdoor space with underfoot padding (or grass) and materials/equipment to support developmentally appealing activity (climbing structures, large rubber balls, chalk, jump ropes, basketball hoops and balls, etc.)

Finally, schools that heal assume that no matter how old the children are, they will require *supportive interaction from adults throughout the day.* Paradoxically, children with traumatic history may present as though they are both older and younger than their years. They may hesitate to ask adults for help, act tough or oblivious, or embody the tone and postures of older kids, teens, or adults. On the other hand, these same children may react to even minor separations, transitions, or disruptions as a disorganized toddler might, without words to express their inner state, even if they have developed a sophisticated vocabulary for other circumstances.

They may crave early level comfort without the psychological home base that allows them to seek that comfort. Therefore, supportive adult–child interactions in the school setting require:

1. An empathic voice tone.
2. Reflective language (mirroring what adult sees and hears with empathy).
3. Comforting and confident presence.
4. Consistent availability re: times of day.
5. Consistent trauma-informed approach among all staff, including lunchroom aids, security guards, and others.
6. Containing aspects/limit-setting articulating cause and effect, communicated with clarity, voiced calmly, and clearly with nonthreatening posture.
7. Opportunities for all staff (lunchroom staff, office and security personnel, etc.) to know all children well and become familiar figures to all children.
8. Understanding and reflecting traumatized children's experience of reexperiencing the past, by acknowledging and helping them to differentiate past from present.

ERASING THE GAP: REDEFINING WHAT COUNTS

The structural components of trauma-informed practice listed above give the school environment an infrastructure for "holding" traumatized children and preventing school from *becoming another* traumatizing environment. The ERP techniques elaborated in the chapters in Part II can empower teachers and school leaders to support this trauma-informed infrastructure of routine, policy, and well thought out physical spaces with interactions and curriculum that address unresolved developmental issues and promote cognitive and social–emotional integration.

If you work in a stressed public school with high numbers of children with traumatic history, you may be wondering how on earth to convince supervisors to consider the emotional needs of children as a greater priority than the test-score outcomes that determine the school's destiny. This conflict is both very real and extremely paradoxical. For instance, there is a well-known connection between poverty and poor testing outcomes (Jensen, 2019; Reardon et al., 2020). There is also a well-established connection between poverty and vulnerability to trauma, as well as poverty and lack of available trauma resources. Schools with the most stressed and traumatized children are the recipients of the *most* extreme pressure from officials to increase their test scores or lose their right to exist, thus exacerbating stress and likely triggering traumatic reactions in their communities!

Typically, administrators receive high levels of pressure for improving test scores from superiors, which gets translated to the teachers, and readily absorbed by children and parents, many of whom *already* carry toxic levels of stress. This additional burden can pose another threat to educational outcomes, as work presented within a high-anxiety atmosphere can decrease access to cognition and increase the risk that children become "allergic" to material that overwhelms them. Testing subjects become the focal point of learning at the expense of other engaging and meaningful areas of learning. In reality, the pressure to produce high scores weakens the infrastructure of trauma-informed care *unless* school leaders, teachers, and parents question the relationship between test-score outcomes in elementary and middle school, and the ability to thrive as learners and citizens as older teens and young adults. Indeed, the "opt out" movement organized by parents has been growing over the years, as parents recognize that their children's curriculum has been shrinking in breadth and depth. This fight, which was initially being waged by middle- and high-income parents, has become more widely supported by parents in all income groups as they become advocates for their children who are not able to find meaning in the score-driven curriculum.

The research on the relationship between poverty, trauma, and testing outcomes is well known, yet pressure to address the *core issues* underlying poor test performance is deflected away from the clear implications for governmental poverty support/action, and instead focused on targeting high-needs schools in debilitating and often trauma-inducing ways. Although it may seem that the connections between poverty, trauma, and testing outcomes are unknown by federal educational policymakers, in fact, federal action in response to community trauma has revealed acknowledgment of those connections. For example, after Hurricane Katrina hit New Orleans, forcing thousands of impoverished children and families to flee the city, the Bush administration offered neighboring towns and states a "pass" on annual testing requirements. This administration was afraid that the recently traumatized and displaced children would score poorly, and counting their scores would cause principals in surrounding areas to hesitate to take them in.

As the most recent sociological research shows, the achievement gap is correlated with learning within an impoverished school and neighborhood community, and is not related to race or ethnicity. Therefore, rather than bring pressure to bear on the schools in impoverished communities, it seems the remedy would need to involve policies that promote socioeconomic integration of schools. Exacerbating pressure within elementary school communities is counterintuitive for improving the educational experiences of traumatized children (Darling-Hammond et al., 2020; Gaffney, 2019). In order to take their responsibility to traumatized children seriously, schools must reevaluate what "counts," and resolve to offer their children a supportive, age-appropriate, engaging, and meaningful educational environment as their core mission. This resolution will require mountains of professional and parental advocacy in order to succeed. However, in the long run, these mountains will be well worth climbing!

Part III

REAL AND PRETEND
FIGHTING FOR CHILDREN'S RIGHT TO WELL-BEING

CHAPTER 7

Freedom to Think, Feel, and Play

Developmental Foundations of Emotional Health

Often, the academic skills of children growing up in other countries and cultures are held in high regard by the corporate funders of score-driven practice. Countries that push early rote mastery, mathematical thinking, and memorization of information are more likely to be held up as worthy of emulation by the corporate world than cultures like Finland, whose early education system emphasizes play and exploration, yet ultimately producing high-achieving adults (Sahlberg, 2015). Paradoxically, the educational methods and outcomes most often held up as exemplary by the U.S. business community come from Asian countries, such as China and Singapore, where freedom of thought is discouraged and government is the only source of information. It is telling that our own Common Core Standards put unprecedented emphasis on factual learning through nonfiction, instead of enrichment through authentic literature and creative arts. What does this prescribed and narrowing vision of education mean for American children, for our democracy, and for the mental health outcomes of our children and families?

FREEDOM TO THINK, FREEDOM TO PLAY

Democracies defend freedom of speech as an individual right, freedom of thought being its theoretical precursor. Since school experience is generally the child's first formal interaction with the larger society outside of family, public schools often encourage children to express their thoughts and opinions through intentional models of democratic process. For example, children in the early grades may be asked to vote for the song they would like to sing at an end-of-year ceremony. Upper-grade children may be asked to vote for a student to represent their class at a student council meeting. Upper elementary, middle school, and high school students may engage in debating, sometimes being asked to take the perspective of another and argue to that point of view. Although some of these practices that encourage student voice are still common, other practices that are foundational for the *development* of complex thought and the development of creative vision in children are disappearing in American public schools. The diminishing of developmentally meaningful opportunities for student voice and creative vision in early childhood and early grade classrooms ultimately can become a threat to democratic process as well as to student mental health.

Even though the Common Core includes a rarely acknowledged section on play and art, score-driven schools let these critical areas of learning, social development, and emotional resilience sit silently within that document. The narrow focus on nonfictional reading and early math skills can inhibit representational and creative thought processes in early childhood, diminish student opportunities for connection as well as self-expression, and ultimately pose challenges to children's mental health.

Research outcomes on the multiple benefits of children's open-ended play are compelling. Studies have connected opportunities for open-ended social play with improvements in self-regulation and the executive functions of memory and thoughtful action (Barker et al., 2014; Thibodeau et al., 2016). A recent paper by the American Pediatric Association (APA) highlights several recent studies connecting open-ended play with toys, versus electronics, with improvements in memory, language comprehension, and the expression of more complex ideas (Yogman et al., 2018). In addition, the paper presents a significant amount of brain research from the study of animals and humans indicating that play offers baby animals and human children a way to avoid becoming overwhelmed by stress. The motivation for this paper was the APA's perception that the diminishing opportunities for play, both in and out of school, were connected to the skyrocketing incidence of anxiety, depression, and suicide rates in older teens and college-aged adults. Other researchers have focused more specifically on the negative mental health effects of high-pressure, no-play early grade classrooms, noting that play is an intrinsically rewarding, self-initiated learning process, while didactic teaching facilitates an externally focused, performance-oriented learning process. One study on the connection between lack of play and the higher incidence of mental health issues states the following:

> Play by definition, is activity controlled and directed by the players; and play, by definition, is directed toward intrinsic rather than extrinsic goals. . . . Our system of constant testing and evaluation in school—which becomes increasingly intense with every passing year—is a system that very clearly substitutes extrinsic rewards and goals for intrinsic ones. It is almost designed to produce anxiety and depression. (Grey, 2010)

Although advocates of score-driven education often articulate their passion for academically oriented early learning as a remedy for educationally underserved children, compelling research shows the opposite to be true, particularly for children with significant amounts of adversity.

Consider the following passages from the APA's statement concerning the role of play in learning:

> In the presence of childhood adversity, play becomes even more important. The mutual joy and shared communication and attunement (harmonious serve and return interactions) that parents and children can experience during play regulate the body's stress response. . . . Early learning and play are fundamentally social activities and fuel the development of language and thought. It has been demonstrated that children playing with toys act like scientists and learn by looking and listening to those around them. However, explicit instructions limit a child's creativity; it is argued that we should let children learn through observation and active engagement rather than passive memorization or direct instruction. (Yogman et al., 2018, p. 1)

Playing from Afar

At the moment of this writing, schoolchildren are learning at home virtually, an avenue of learning that is more effective for older children than for their younger schoolmates. Bank Street Emotionally Responsive Practice (ERP) staff virtually visit many lower-grade classes in New York City as teachers do their best to connect with children and engage them remotely, as shown in the following vignette.

In a 2nd-grade class in a stressed area of the city where the incidence of COVID-19 is high and resources are low, children have their morning meeting from their homes. The teacher, Ms. T., is competing with ambient noise coming from full households, as many children have not mastered the technique of muting themselves, then unmuting when they want to talk. A child raises his hand and speaks in a sad voice:

Charles: My uncle and my cousin died from COVID-19. My uncle died this morning, and my cousin died yesterday.

Some children start to cry. Ms. T. feels at a loss to help with the sadness, fear, and grief that this story brings up, especially since she is not physically present. She attempts to contain the emotion by asking children what they can do to make sure they stay safe from COVID-19.

In unison, they reply, "Stay at home and wash your hands." "Wear a mask if you have to go outside."

Ms. T. seems relieved. "Very good!" she says. The children stop crying, but look exhausted, and distracted. Adrianne, the ERP consultant visiting the class, uses reflective language to comment on what she sees and hears coming from the children.

Adrianne: It sounds like you have a lot of thoughts and feelings about COVID-19. I am wondering what you know about it.

Many hands go up.

"It came from China when someone ate a bat and got sick."
"It kills old people, and now it can kill children."
"If you go outside, you might die."
"If you go outside you might get stung by a killer bee who has COVID-19."

Ms. T.: Some of those things are partially true, but some are not. Maybe, we should make a list of questions that you have about COVID-19, and then we can do some research to find the answers.

Ms. T.'s comment contains the anxiety in the room somewhat. Children no longer feel alone, but are still looking fragile and fearful.

Adrianne: I have an idea! Go and get a Teddy Bear or another stuffed animal that you love.

The children happily scatter to retrieve their stuffed animals.

Adrianne: I am thinking that your animals are very sad about Charles's news. They may have also heard scary things about COVID-19 on the radio or on TV, and they might feel scared or worried. They might even have a tummyache or a headache! What can you do to help them feel safe and well? Everyone get some things that you think will help your stuffy, and play about making your stuffy feel better for 15 minutes. You can be anyone you want to be in your play, or you can decide to just be you. Then, we'll come back and share what happened in the play.

Once again children scatter, some returning to play in front of the screen, and some coming back only when the 15 minutes were up.

Adrianne: How are your stuffed animals feeling now? Everyone can have a turn to tell us what you and your stuffy played about.

Almost every child raised their hand, eager to share.

Charles: I was the doctor and I took care of my bear with a special soup, and now he feels much better.

Mia: I was a wizard and I made a magic potion and rubbed it on my Teddy Bear's head, and that made his headache go away!

Joshua: I was an inventor, and I invented a machine that killed COVID-19! That made my stuffy feel safe again.

LaKeisha: I was a scientist, and I mixed chemicals together in one of those clear tubes like on TV, and it came out with a liquid. Then, I poured it into a syringe, and then I gave my Doggie a shot with it that made him into a "super dog." Now he is so strong he can't catch any diseases!

Adrianne: It sounds like you found some great ways to make your stuffed animals healthy! They won't have to worry so much now that since they have you around to take such good care of them.

Ms. T: Does anybody know a name for what LaKeisha invented to protect her dog? I'll give you a hint! You already have to have some of these kinds of shots to be able to start school.

Children called out some guesses.

"Needles!"

"Booster shots!"

"Vaccinations!"

"Vaccines!"

Ms. T.: Yes! Right now there are scientists all over the world who are working on making a vaccine that will prevent people from getting sick with COVID-19.

Mia: I heard that on the news!

Ms. T.: Did you know that there were other sicknesses that used to be very dangerous a long time ago, but we don't get them anymore because someone invented a vaccine to protect us? If you talk to your grandparents or great-grandparents, you can ask them if they remember those times.

Miguel: My cousin caught the measles, and my mom was yelling at my aunt because my aunt forgot to take my cousin to the doctor to get the vaccine.

Adrianne looked at the children on the screen. Their worn, anxious, fearful expressions had disappeared. The children were attentive and engaged, and they appeared less vulnerable.

Later, Ms. T. and Adrianne collaborated to brainstorm ways to follow the emergent themes that had come up in the children's play. These could be followed up within science, social studies, and literacy curricula where the history of inventing cures and preventing illness could be explored. Children could also be invited to create their own "play cures," considering ingredients that might make good remedies for both a physical hurt and an emotional hurt.

Ms. T. and Adrianne talked with the school's social worker about what kinds of support the school could offer to Charles and his family. Tragically, the likelihood that more of the children would be experiencing multiple losses was high, since many children in this school community were living in crowded, multigeneration households.

Additional invitations for play as a potential integrator of difficult experience were woven into the remote learning experience for Ms. T.'s children over the months left in the school year, addressing the reality that many children were likely to feel isolated with trauma and loss during this tragic time.

Play Within the Classroom Community: A Preventive Measure

Children who become flooded with sadness, fear, or anger frequently feel helpless to attend to their teachers or classmates as these strong emotions wash over them. Those children who withdraw from the group when this happens may go unnoticed. Those children who fight to emerge from the emotional waters by thrashing and pushing, or acting out in ways that make others feel as vulnerable and helpless as they do, get their names put on "red" on the classroom behavior chart.

In human development, all children and adults have both positive and negative thoughts, feelings, and impulses. Many factors impact the ability of children and adults to integrate all of these in order to keep a healthy emotional balance, including prior life experiences, physiology (constitutional factors), and the experience of relationship support for the brain development that allows for emotional integration and self-regulation (refer to Chapter 3). Likewise, many factors impact a child's ability to take in and retain new learning, to find learning engaging and meaningful, and to maintain focus and be motivated to follow through on increasingly complex demands. Therefore, there is almost always a continuum of functioning within a school environment, both *among* the children in the school community and *within* each member of that community.

For example, the same child who is a precocious reader in kindergarten may be less socially astute than one of his peers who is not yet reading.

An upper-grade student who is a math wiz is confounded by the poetry that the class is analyzing. The 2nd-grader who wins the school spelling bee can't wait his turn in the lunch line without pushing and shoving. If this sounds like a typical classroom constellation, it is! Yet, it is rare to find a school community that organizes its mission and identity around acknowledging this typical presentation of human diversity. The myth of perfection as the ideal is dangerously persistent.

Our schools and our students are often pressured to engage in work to prove their excellence, or alternatively to fall short and therefore fail. There is little comfort with or mention of thriving somewhere in between. The "excellent" student feels pressure to maintain her excellence at all costs. When she experiments with putting her energies elsewhere and her grades respond by showing a B+ instead of an A, she is overwhelmed with guilt and anxiety. The "failing" student cannot imagine getting to that faraway point of excellence, especially if his talents don't ever seem to "count" in numerical terms. He acts out in reaction.

We know that there is a space *in between* the demand for focused attention to curriculum that may not be meaningful to stressed children and waiting for the dam to break so that the whole classroom is flooded by enacted anger and fear. That space exists when there are invitations to connect, play, create, and invent throughout the school day (refer to Chapter 5). Without those invitations, schoolchildren who struggle to manage their negative emotions in the classroom can sink further and further into a feeling of worthlessness each time their name is put on "red" on the classroom behavior chart. To these children "red" means "I am bad and worthless." To an emotionally overwhelmed child, his "choices" might be perceived as either putting his head down on the desk so that no one can see him or knocking over the behavior chart easel in a fit of rage! Most likely, the child will act to fight the "bad and worthless" feeling, or succumb to it,

Neither option will get the child to "green."

Although adults often perceive "bad" behavior to be a choice, the opposite choice being "good" behavior which is just as accessible, the children who struggle with their stresses experience no such option. Indeed, generally speaking, the alternative to acting-out behavior for children who lose their emotional balance is dissolving into tears, emotional withdrawal, or depression. In the long run, interactive feelings charts (see the Appendix, Handout 4) outdo behavior charts for promoting an emotionally healthy classroom climate, as they reflect a range of emotions without assigning more value to one than the others, and don't shame children who are vulnerable to acting out their emotional pain, a practice that adds insult to injury (Blachly & Dean, 2019).

"Good Guys" and "Bad Guys"

When young children have time, space, and support to engage in pretend play, themes involving "good guys" and "bad guys" often emerge.
Although adults may have varied reactions to this kind of play, or impose
their own moral or sociopolitical views when interpreting its value, this
play theme for 3–6-year-olds has endured over time. When children begin to draw and write, and then when skill levels allow them to become
fluent enough to write expressively, the "good guy"/"bad guy" themes
are prevalent in creative efforts as well as in their interpretations of reality
in preschool to 2nd grade. When given space, time, and support for play,
playful thoughts, and the creation of symbol and metaphor, children use
these opportunities to better integrate their own positive and negative
feelings and impulses with the "good guy"/"bad guy" metaphor. The
play, drawing, and story writing help them to emerge as "OK guys," or as
people who have a better balance of both positive and negative thoughts
and feelings.

When the identity issues prevalent in early adolescence resurface, this
foundational play in early childhood can allow older children to return to
integrating these parts of themselves on a more intentional level, as they
begin to imagine themselves as older teenagers and young adults.

The Tool of Metaphor and Connection in the Healing Classroom

Well-protected children initially make sense of the world using both fantasy and reality factors, and only very gradually interpret experience based
on thoughtful, conceptually sound conclusions. Parents and teachers are
called on to serve as interpreters for children aged 3 to 12, as they gradually take in more and more from the big world outside of home. Strong
parent–child relationships and strong teacher–child relationships help to
protect children from overwhelming reality and offer small world ways of
understanding big issues little by little.

In ERP classrooms, teachers know that the offer needs to include
structured opportunities for the creation of story and metaphor in addition to time and space for open-ended play. Vivian Paley's (1991) story-
acting technique can be a useful tool offering these opportunities.

Story acting asks children to dictate or write their own stories, which
are then acted out by the authors and their peers. The invitation for story
is open-ended, but to invite fantasy in, having children begin their stories with "Once upon a time . . ." is suggested. Consider the following
stories, dictated and enacted by 5-year-olds as part of their story-acting

Figure 7.1 The Robber Who Ate Soup

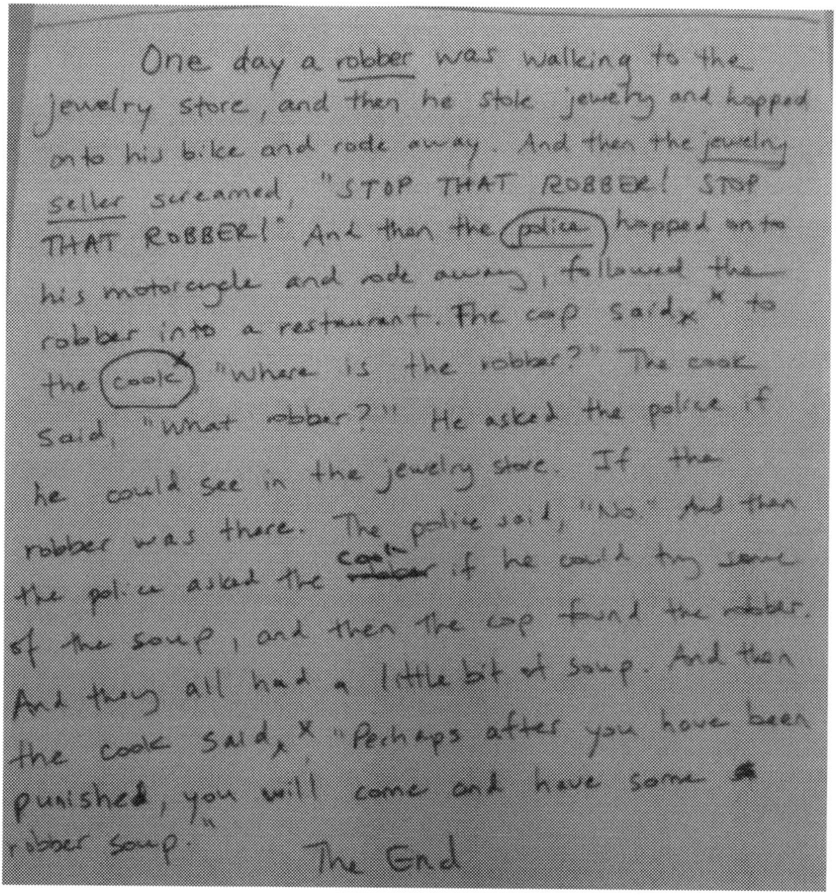
One day a robber was walking to the jewelry store, and then he stole jewelry and hopped onto his bike and rode away. And then the jewelry seller screamed, "STOP THAT ROBBER! STOP THAT ROBBER!" And than the police hopped onto his motorcycle and rode away, followed the robber into a restaurant. The cop said to the cook "Where is the robber?" The cook said, "What robber?" He asked the police if he could see in the jewelry store. If the robber was there. The police said, "No." And than the police asked the cook if he could try some of the soup, and then the cop found the robber. And they all had a little bit of soup. And then the cook said, "Perhaps after you have been punished, you will come and have some robber soup."

The End

"One day a robber was walking to the jewelry store, and then he stole jewelry and hopped onto his bike and rode away. And then the jewelry seller screamed, 'Stop that robber! Stop that robber!' And then the police hopped onto his motorcycle and rode away, followed the robber into a restaurant. The cop said to the cook, 'Where is the robber?' The cook said, 'What robber?' He asked the police if he could see in the jewelry store. If the robber was there. The police said, 'No.' And then the police asked the cook if he could try some of the soup, and then the cop found the robber. And they all had a little bit of soup. And then the cook said, 'Perhaps after you have been punished, you will come and have some robber soup.'"

Figure 7.2 The Princess Who Lived in a Forest

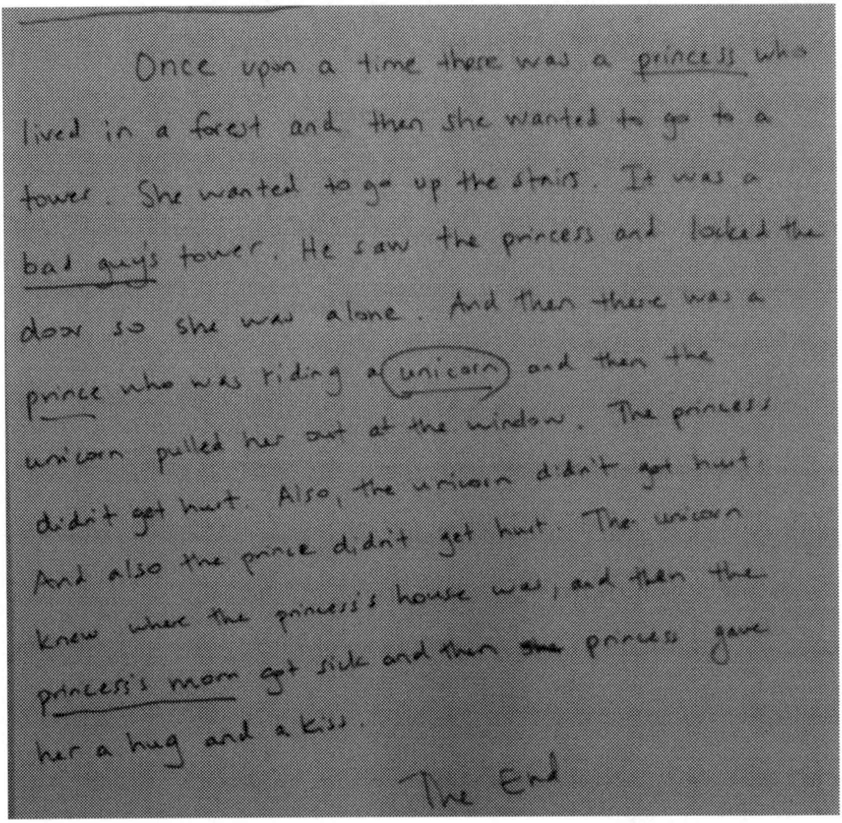
Once upon a time there was a princess who
lived in a forest and then she wanted to go to a
tower. She wanted to go up the stairs. It was a
bad guy's tower. He saw the princess and locked the
door so she was alone. And then there was a
prince who was riding a unicorn and then the
unicorn pulled her out at the window. The princess
didn't get hurt. Also, the unicorn didn't get hurt
And also the prince didn't get hurt. The unicorn
knew where the princess's house was, and then the
princess's mom got sick and then ~~she~~ princess gave
her a hug and a kiss.
The End

"Once upon a time there was a princess who lived in a forest and then she wanted to go to a tower. She wanted to go up the stairs. It was a bad guy's tower. He saw the princess and locked the door so she was alone. And then there was a prince who was riding a unicorn and then the unicorn pulled her out at the window. The princess didn't get hurt. Also, the unicorn didn't get hurt. And also, the prince didn't get hurt. The unicorn knew where the princess's house was, and then the princess's mom got sick and the prince gave her a hug and a kiss. The end."

curriculum (see Figures 7.1 and 7.2 for the children's original dictations as transcribed by their teacher).

Both of these 5-year-olds used their story writing and acting invitations to symbolize the power and powerlessness issues that are typical for this age group. The theme of "good guy" and "bad guy" permeate both stories, each author using different metaphors to symbolize their attempts to integrate the positive and negative desires and emotions that all children carry. In the first story, the "bad guy" is a robber who robs a jewelry store and is caught by a police officer and a cook who then all have soup together. Themes of authority and nurture are woven into the narrative that allows for a just but hopeful resolution. In the second story, a princess is locked in a "bad guy's" tower until a prince on a unicorn makes a daring rescue. The author is very quick to assure us that no one got hurt as a result of the princess's need for adventure. Themes of separation and autonomy are embodied here, and ultimately provide the princess's mom with an additional source of comfort. Both stories involve conflict and action, and both stories are compelling to other children as they are acted out, since the developmental themes resonate with the age group and allow the children to connect around ambivalence rather than feel shame or isolation.

ONCE UPON A TIME AND THE FREEDOM TO LEARN BY PLAYING

Vivian Paley's story-acting technique serves multiple purposes for the young learner. It allows children to see their dictated stories in written form, and then gives them the power to bring their stories to life by acting them out within their community of peers. Storytelling and eventually story writing become a voice for their own thoughts and feelings, and are intrinsically motivating and compelling. Emotional energy that comes from young children's developmental conflicts and confusing life experiences has a prosocial place to go, as this form of self-expression fits well within the containing structure of the literacy curriculum. Inviting and appreciating fantasy as well as reality factors in the classroom offers emotional release, social opportunity, and an alternative to acting out when conflicts are too difficult to articulate.

In order for teachers to offer such learning opportunities to the children in their classrooms, they have to feel free to teach intuitively, using the sciences of relationship-based learning, brain development, play and creative discovery, and trauma-informed care to guide the evolution of classroom practice. Once upon a time, this was possible. In order to ensure the well-being and competence of our children in the 21st century, it must become possible again.

CHAPTER 8

Umbrellas for Teachers and Leaders

In order to remain empathic and responsive to children and parents, teachers and leaders need "good mirrors" for their important work. The dangers of leaving the emotional well-being and moral support of teachers and school leaders to chance are evident, particularly in high-needs school communities. Statistics reveal a destabilizing teacher turnover rate of 16%, with 44% of teachers leaving the classroom after 5 years (Ingersoll et al., 2018). Math and science teachers leave high poverty schools at rates 70% higher than higher-income schools (Carver-Thomas & Darling-Hammond, 2017). The openings created by high rates of attrition are most likely filled by new and less experienced teachers, which are harder and harder to find as enrollment in colleges of education has plummeted over the last years. Many of the young people who used to "raise their hands" to become educators put their hands down when the freedom to teach was curtailed, curriculum became micromanaged, and the profession was painted as incompetent. Scarier still may be the numbers of teachers who stay in place but cannot maintain empathy or connection with the children they teach, as they try to survive in settings that have zero tolerance for anything other than score-driven teaching.

Emotionally Responsive Practice (ERP) offers teachers an invitation for self-expression, connection, and integration of classroom experiences, parallel to those offered to children and parents in the ERP-informed school. Teacher support groups are considered a critical component of ERP, as teachers bare witness to the complex lives of their students, manage the pressures of their own lives, and struggle to make sense of the overwhelming emotional reactions that are often evoked in classrooms.

Although practitioners in most professions can maintain a comfortable distance from their own childhood experiences, teachers do not have that luxury. The classroom can be a highly evocative and sometimes confusing place, as the life stories of both children and teachers weave together to form the classroom dynamic. Teacher support groups can provide a nonjudgmental venue for sorting out past from present, supporting teacher mental health, and fighting a frequently felt sense of inadequacy that comes from being expected to do more than is possible on any given day.

Essentially, teacher support groups that focus on teachers' felt experiences can decrease the emotional isolation of classroom life, enhance connection to other professionals who know the intensity of the work, and give educators access to emotional support within community. Equally valuable to the preservation of teacher mental health is the opportunity to have reality affirmed by those who are closest to the work. There is enormous relief in having a good mirror for classroom life, when distorted images of teaching and learning abound in both fictional and allegedly factual media accounts every day.

"LITTLE SELF" COMES IN

ERP teacher support groups generally begin with an invitation to the teacher's "little self," meaning that they begin by creating an avenue of connection to the child in school that grew up to be a teacher. Because teachers are a part of the "inner circle" of adults who contribute to children's sense of competence and self-worth, it is important to offer teachers a parallel opportunity for connection to their own stories as schoolchildren who were once dependent on parents and teachers in their own lives. As in parent work, the power of intergenerational aspects of caring for children for hours every day can have a life of its own. Bringing teachers' childhood experiences to light can help them more intentionally consider what traditional approaches and classroom practices they want to "hand down" to the generation of children in their current classrooms, as well as those approaches and practices that they want to consciously prevent from being "handed down."

For an initial activity with a teacher support group, the ERP facilitator provides flat wooden "little people" made by craft companies, along with markers, colored pencils, crayons, and sometimes cloth, glue sticks, and WIKI Stix. The facilitator invites the teachers present to use the "little people" and art materials to represent the children they once were, in the grade that they are now teaching. When all the participants have taken time to create an image of themselves as children, they are invited to introduce their "big self" and "little self" to the group. A sample introduction protocol follows:

2nd-Grade Teacher—Hi. I am Renate, and I teach 2nd grade.
This is "Little Renate." Little Renate loved school, but she didn't

like to go home at the end of the day. Her parents got divorced in 2nd grade, and her mom went back to work, so the house felt sad and lonely.

4th-Grade Teacher—Hello, everyone. My name is Steven, and I teach 4th grade. My class is really demanding, and it takes all my energy just to keep things going. This is "Little Steven" in 4th grade. Unlike my kids now, Little Steven was always well behaved at school, and wanted to show the teacher that he was really smart. But the other kids didn't really like him, and sometimes they were mean to him. But at least he got good grades.

Kindergarten Teacher—Hi. My name is Kendra, and I teach kindergarten. This is "Little Kendra." Little Kendra was only 5 years old when her mom died, the summer before kindergarten. No one knew what to say to her when they found out. The teacher never mentioned it, even though there were special days when parents were supposed to come to school, and most kids' mothers were there. "Little Kendra" cried every night, even though her grandma told her that her mom still loved her from heaven. At school, she was in a daze and ended up repeating kindergarten.

Pre-K Teacher—Hello, everyone. I am Rhee, and I am teaching pre-K for the first time. I always taught upper grades before. It's confusing, you know, because I am supposed to let kids play after years of play being forbidden. This is "Little Rhee." She did not go to pre-K, because there was no such thing in her country, but this is Little Rhee in 1st grade. She had to sit at a small desk all day long and memorize. If she got bored and looked out of the window, the teacher came over and slammed her desk with a book.

When every teacher has had a chance to introduce the adult and child self, the facilitator invites the group to share how it felt to think about their "little selves" in context of their work. This is usually a lively and engaging discussion, with several teachers participating. Eventually, participants are asked how well they thought their teacher at the time knew the "little self" they had introduced. Had their teacher at the time made life and learning more or less hopeful? In retrospect, what else had their little selves needed from their teacher?

Bringing teacher's "little selves" into the room serves multiple purposes for the introductory group process. The stories create connection between teacher participants who may identify with many of the child-hood stories they are hearing. The stories create connection between the adults that the participants have become, and the children they once were. Holding their "little selves" in mind as they consider their own classroom practice helps to prevent difficult history from repeating with-out the teacher's permission. The invitation to connect with the "little self" within community becomes a relief, since classroom life is likely to evoke "little self" reactions that must be fought off so that they re-main invisible to others. Teachers often feel the stress of this unacknowl-edged but exhausting fight, sometimes manifesting in physical symptoms and emotional fatigue. Teacher support groups can provide a time and space to protect teachers from their own classroom-connected emotional storms.

MORE THAN WORDS: STORY, MAGIC, AND METAPHOR IN TEACHER SUPPORT

After the introductory teacher support session, ERP teacher support groups follow emergent themes that come from the group itself. Although participants may want to make verbal sharing the center of their time together, there are always facilitator invitations for creative expression that may offer participants other opportunities to give complex and over-whelming emotional experience a comfortable "place to live." Although these invitations for artistic expression are often met with incredulous reactions and initial refusal, they almost always become a surprising re-source, even for teachers who describe themselves as "not artistic." At the following midyear support session the facilitator's agenda is to follow emergent themes and invite deeper exploration of common ground is-sues that emerge from group conversation. These invitations may include creative expression through various expressive arts modalities.

Ten teachers are seated around the table in a small meeting room, and two are sprawled out on coaches surrounding the crowded table. The facilitator is also at the table with a mountain of art supplies in front of her and a sign-in sheet to send around. These particular teachers represent neighborhood schools whose school leaders find it worthwhile to cover their staff in order to allow teachers to avail themselves of this monthly support.

> *Facilitator:* Good morning! Anyone want to bring us up to date on a
> story shared last time we met?

*Two teachers say "Yes!" simultaneously, then laugh at the parallel
between themselves and the eager students in their classrooms.*

Tina: OK. You can go, but first we have to say, "Jinx! Buy me a coke!"

Jenn: Thanks. I wanted to tell everyone what happened with the
     scary parent who insisted on coming with us on the fieldtrip to
     the museum even though the buses were full.

Rick: Did you end up taking her?

Jenn (nods): I did! She called the district office, the superintendent,
     and the local news station and said she had the right to go
     anywhere that her child was required to go! We finally just
     agreed.

Eileen: How was it?

Jenn: Interesting! I was afraid she would be a lot to handle, since she
     always seems to have a problem with whatever I ask her for, and
     she has a booming voice that scares the kids if she is upset about
     something. But when we went into the museum where the giant
     stuffed wild animals were, I could see that it was she who was
     afraid. She kept her son very close to her, and the two of them
     stayed very close to me at the front of the line. She looked
     dazed and never said a word.

Facilitator: Maybe she went to the museum with her class as a child
     when she was too young to sort out real from pretend, and was
     terrified by what she saw. Maybe her teachers didn't give the kids
     clarity about what they were taking in, or why they were there.

Annie: That happened to me when I was a kid! They took me to the
     circus and didn't tell me what I would be seeing there. I
     screamed the whole time because I thought the elephant was
     going to eat me up! I still get tense when I take my own kids to
     the circus!

Jake: It's even harder for people who are growing up now
     surrounded by computer-generated images of scary creatures
     coming to life on every screen. Someone has to interpret what
     kids are taking in to help them sort things out!

Jenn: I ended up feeling enormous relief and empathy. Relief that
     she wasn't scary to be with, and empathy for her commitment
     to protect her son, even though she felt so unsafe herself.

Group nodding, then silence.

Tina: Can I share? This is the story about the kid whose dad was
     arrested and still in prison awaiting trial. His son, a boy in my

kindergarten class who had been semistable, became suddenly violent and impossible to manage. He tried to break the window by punching it with his fist, threw over tables, and lunged at my face with a pencil pointed at my eyes. If you remember, his explosion of rage had just started before I was here last time, and I was freaking out!

Rick: Did they call EMS? That's my school's "go to" when a kid freaks out.

Tina: No. In the end, we actually used ERP tools to solve it. My ERP consultant helped me. We did Story Gathering with the mom, to understand how things had gone down, and what my student actually saw, which was horrifying. In all likelihood, the dad was innocent, but being held on a technicality (because there may be immigration issues as well). Anyway, we talked to the little boy about how angry he was about what happened to his dad, and how angry *anyone* would be who saw that happen, and then he couldn't even be with his dad to talk about it! We made him two books. One was the story of him and his dad in photographs that his mom provided for us. The other one was a book about things he could do when he felt angry. We also did a class-wide affect and emotion study, so that all kids were able to own and express a range of feelings. It worked! He is connected to me and to the other kids, and sometimes very sad, but not aggressive.

Jenn: And how are you?

Tina: I can't believe how REALLY close I came to calling it quits after that first week! I was terrified that he would really hurt himself or somebody else and I would be held responsible! I cried when I got home from school every night for 2 weeks. Now, I feel like I am actually the right person to be with this little guy at this painful time in his life, and even better, I know that I CAN be with him, and that he can be part of the group.

Facilitator: Why did the ERP tools work for Tina and this little boy? They don't *always* work so dramatically . . .

Chrystal: Because Tina respected the feelings behind his behavior, as well as the story that caused the explosion! She acknowledged what was really going on for this child. That way, he wasn't alone with it anymore.

Jenn: And she brought the mother in, and she became part of the support in this situation.

Tina (nodding): After he stopped acting out the rage, he started to play about what happened, using the little people and the community worker figures in the block area. He builds a lot of jails, and at the end, he always lets the prisoners go home to their families. I think it really helps him to play out the ending he needs to happen. He feels more powerful.

Facilitator: Let's use the rest of our time to create a symbolic solution to something in your own practice that keeps you from feeling powerful. Use the art materials to create something that holds or communicates your frustration or conflict, or maybe can become a metaphor that holds both moments of desperation and moments of hope. When you're done, you can share what you create and explain the symbolism. I think I will suggest using the WIKI Stix since we are getting short on time . . .

Participants pass the materials around and take what they want. They have been in the group long enough to accept these materials without protest or disclaimers about their own lack of artistic abilities. There is a shift from group energy to an inward focus, as people think about representing what is going on for them, and allow the expressive art to have a life of its own. Little by little, colorful wax-covered strings were being woven into shapes and patterns, becoming images that were unique to each creator.

Facilitator: When you finish, feel free to share the symbolism of your creation.

Jake: This (pointing to the fringes on his colorful weave) is my magic carpet. I tell the kids to sit on the rug a million times a day, and that brings our group together. One little girl always falls asleep if we are there for any length of time. I used to try to wake her. Then I thought about how exhausted she seems every morning, like she had willed herself to stay up all night, maybe like a night watchman. Our social worker thinks there might be serious issues there. I finally decided to let her sleep for now. It's true that I can't teach a sleeping child, and that's frustrating. And I am afraid the AP will come by and get on my case. On the other hand, I think the group feels safe and protective for this kid, so she can allow herself to sleep, and that becomes my magical power. It's like being able to feed a starving child with invisible food. If she can sleep, maybe she can dream. Maybe she hears everything we are saying, and it soaks in somehow.

Tina: It's Maslow's hierarchy of needs! Sleep comes before subtraction! I might as well share mine now. (Tina's creation looked like a series of various sized and colored boulders on a flat, multicolored circle.) I was still thinking about my transformed little boy, and when Jenn asked how *I* was doing, it brought me back to how I felt before we helped him. How scared I was. I felt like one of these (points) little pebbles, trying to survive this giant rage-full monster (points to the giant, looming, red shape) who threatened to destroy everything I worked so hard to create! Then, the little boy's story came to light (points to yellow ball on the edge), and it became clear that *he* was the one trying to survive a monster who threatened his precious family, and all of a sudden, he was small enough to hold. (Tina folded her creation so everything was now inside.)

Facilitator: Tina's story has so much in it. One thing that came to me is how few people outside of the profession would imagine that teaching lower-grade children could be as scary as it sometimes is. If anyone feels like following that theme next time we meet, we can. Use your journal to jot down anything that comes to you that seems connected to the emergent themes that arose today, and make sure you have the date for our next group meeting.

Group members gather materials and coats, and walk out together, talking among themselves as the facilitator collects her materials.

ACCESS AND SUPPORT FOR STRENGTHENING THE INNER CIRCLE

Teachers leave the classroom for many reasons, stress and burnout being two of the most prevalent (Jacobson, 2016). Midyear departures from the classroom are especially disruptive, as children struggle to regain equilibrium when their inner circle of important adults is suddenly missing an important link in its holding capacity. ERP school communities know that teaching is a multifaceted art and science, requiring a very human and sometimes, superhuman, effort to reach and teach groups of children with a variety of talents and challenges. In order to remain strong and present, teachers need universal access to support that is tailored to their professional lives. Teacher support groups work to provide both a good mirror for the reality of the work as well as a safe place for teachers to make emotional sense of their classroom experiences within community.

Recently, focus groups of teachers whose schools are, or have been, involved in ERP met as a courtesy to me to offer advice concerning this book's content. The topic of teacher support groups arose. Multiple participants began to voice the same spontaneous conclusion:

"Without the groups, I would NOT still be in the classroom!"

"If my school stopped participating, I would use my sick days and show up anyway!"

"If my 'little self' had never been invited into my professional life, my 'big self' would be long gone!"

Under the umbrella of the monthly (or bimonthly) support group, caring and talented teachers are protected. When we can protect our talented teachers, we protect the vulnerable children who depend on them every day.

When children and teachers live with false narratives about what constitutes success and failure in school, feelings of inadequacy, anxiety, and exhaustion are easily engendered, and can overwhelm their ability to remain authentically engaged. Providing an "accurate mirror" for the experiences that teachers have in their lives at school can improve their capacity to provide hopeful and supportive relationship-based education for children. These "umbrellas" are an essential component of schools that heal.

Epilogue

I began writing this book in July 2019, knowing that I would be on sabbatical for the following semester, which was designed to allow me to focus on writing. What I didn't foresee was that 10 days after I had more or less finished the writing and returned to work, COVID-19 would close the country down, including all of our schools. ERP suddenly needed to translate via Zoom and other virtual platforms, and the need to support teachers and children struggling with this new reality and the subsequent COVID-related losses became all consuming. Wanting to include some of what we had experienced during the time that New York City was the epicenter of the pandemic, I went back to the manuscript and was able to revise and rework some of the content to include a little bit of our early experiences within the context of COVID-19. In mid-May, the manuscript was off to a colleague for formatting help prior to being sent back to the publisher in time for final edits.

On May 25, George Floyd was murdered by police in Minneapolis. The imagery of this horrific event, and the proactive response organized by Black Lives Matter, resulted in a groundswell of protest and support for people of color who have died unjustly at the hands of law enforcement. All of these events were present in the minds and hearts of children in the last few weeks of the virtual school year. They will likely still be present when children return in the fall, requiring teachers to partner with children to help them make sense of what they have taken in, and to support their strength and resilience.

On July 20, 2020, iconic civil rights leader and congressman John Lewis died of cancer at age 80. His death was a monumental loss at a critical time. Days before he died, John Lewis attended a Black Lives Matter demonstration to see young people engaging in the kind of activism he had led so many times in his life. He was deeply inspired. He wrote an essay to be read at his funeral, including the reminder that "Democracy is not a state. It is an act that each generation must do its part to build, what we called 'The Beloved Community,' a nation and world society at peace with itself" (Lewis, 2020).

In a tribute to John Lewis, *New York Times* columnist Jamelle Bouie compared John Lewis's philosophy about democracy to the philosophy of John Dewey, referenced in Chapter 1 of this book (Bouie, 2020). Both men were passionate about education, John Lewis often crediting his lifelong love of reading to a favorite elementary school teacher. Both men were authors, addressing the importance of youth participation in the creation of democracy. Indeed, John Dewey believed that experience-based, participatory education not only provided children with a strong conceptual basis for learning, but allowed them to experience democracy within the classroom at a young age.

John Dewey saw a democratic society as one that gave its children an opportunity to develop their "distinctive capacities" to their full potential, so that these capacities could be used in service of their communities as they grew up. John Lewis fought relentlessly to make those opportunities available to children of color, and taught youth by example to fight for civil rights and human dignity, and to never give up. Among his publications is a series of graphic novels for young people about the power of activism. Both men made sure that their beliefs and legacy would survive them.

Teachers, school leaders, and school social workers who are working during this time of COVID-19 may be desperately searching for evidence that the ethics of a caring democracy embodied by these great men can be "brought back to life." Educators are watching their students and their families suffer, while school and other social service budgets shrink without government rescue. Many in the field feel helpless and demoralized. They see the results of systemic racism and classism that create barriers to their students' access to nutritious food, health care, and housing, and leaves their families vulnerable to illness and loss. They find themselves suddenly facing risks to their own health and well-being especially if their government mandates a return to the classroom before a vaccine is available. They find themselves left out of the democratic process that will take their needs and the needs of their students into account.

Those educators who find a way to stay present in the lives of children through these years and beyond may not realize the strength of their contributions. Those teachers who offer children a good mirror in the classroom ensure both an emotionally and culturally responsive learning environment, as they reflect children's identity and personhood in a positive light. Those schools that give children a voice within the social milieu of the classroom offer them early experience in creating and supporting democratic processes. Those teachers who cherish, nurture, and teach in responsive and loving ways create a classroom-based version of what John

Lewis called "Beloved Community." Those school leaders who cherish, nurture, and lead the adults who spend hours every day in the company of children create a school-based version of what John Lewis called "Beloved Community." These educators create a just society in miniature. They create schools that heal.

Appendix

GUIDE TO CHOOSING REFLECTIVE BOOKS

Choose books that address the issues that are "common ground" for many of the children in the group. If the books have the qualities listed below, they will lend themselves to the reflective process.

1. Does the book reflect developmental issues that resonate with the age group?

2. Does the book reflect life experiences that are familiar to the children in the room?

3. Does the book provide a "good mirror" for the children who are listening, by accurately reflecting their experiences either directly or through metaphor, and portraying people like them in a positive light?

4. Does the story include ambivalence, acknowledge conflict, and allow children to use both fantasy and reality factors to integrate content?

5. Does the story invite exploration of complex dynamics rather than dictate behavior?

Handout 2
Early Childhood and Lower-Grade Children

GUIDE TO INVITING REFLECTIVE LITERACY
FOLLOW-UP ACTIVITIES

Discussion Prompts:

What did you think about the story?

What did the story remind you of?

Does anyone else want to say something about that?

Drawing Invitations:

If you would like to draw and tell your own story about _____, get
    some paper and crayons and start to draw.

When you're finished, let me know and I will come over to listen to
    your drawing story, and write your words down.

Writing Invitations:

You know a lot about _____.

Or . . . you have a lot of ideas/feelings about ____.

Use your journal to write more about it.

Or . . . get some paper to write your own story about anything that the
    book reminded you of.

Play Invitations:

Put theme-related materials in the dramatic play corner to invite
    children to explore themes through play.

Introduce story acting, inviting children to dictate or write "Once Upon
    a Time" stories; then choose peers to help them act those stories out.

Upper-Grade Children

Discussion Prompts:

Did the story we read remind you of anything else that we read? Explain.

Where did that story take you as you listened?

How did you feel about the ending?

What makes this a good fit for kids your age? (If you agree.)

What makes this not quite right for kids your age? (If you agree.)

Writing Invitations:

Write your own story that connects to the story that we read.

After you are finished, write a paragraph or make a drawing that illustrates the connection between the two stories.

Write a poem that explores one of the themes that came out of the story.

Drama Invitations:

How could we dramatize the themes that came out of the story in creative ways that are just right for kids your age?

Work with a small group to write a script that you can act out together for the rest of the class.

What did those mini-plays have in common? Did they communicate the same themes or different themes?

Art Invitations:

Design a mural that communicates your feelings about the story.

Make a painting that brings a powerful part of the story to life.

Handout 3

PLAN FOR INTEGRATING EXPRESSIVE INVITATIONS
INTO CONTAINING PRACTICES

1. Make a classroom schedule of routines and subjects in column 1.

_____	_____
_____	_____
_____	_____
_____	_____
_____	_____

2. After each subject/routine listed above, write down in column 2 one or more expressive invitations that can be integrated into the item on the schedule. Expressive invitations can include discussion, drawing, acting, play, building, writing, singing, and dancing.

3. Revisit this process weekly as a way of ensuring that invitations for self-expression are integrated into children's day-to-day learning experiences on an ongoing basis.

Handout 4

GUIDE TO MAKING INTERACTIVE FEELINGS CHARTS

1. Attach photographs, drawings, or cut out pictures that represent a variety of emotional states to a poster board. Feature fewer feeling states for use with very young children, but make sure that happy, sad, angry, and scared are included. For older children, represent a larger variety of feelings. Label the feelings pictured. Leave space under or next to pictures and feeling words.

2. Laminate the poster board or cover it with contact paper.

3. Attach Velcro dots or cloth or paper pockets underneath or next to each feeling word.

4. Have children's name tags, symbols, or flat wooden people sticks in a basket near the chart, so that they can be used to indicate what a child is feeling at the time of use.

5. Integrate the feelings chart into the classroom routine, as part of arrival, meeting, or other daily practices. In addition, invite children to use the chart to express feelings that they are having trouble verbalizing.

References

Achilles, C. M., & Dun Schiffman, C. (2012, October). Class-size policy: The star experiment and related class-size studies. *NCPEA Policy Brief, 1*(2). https://files.eric.ed.gov/fulltext/ED540485.pdf

Ainsworth, M. D. S., Belhar, M. C., & Waters, E. (1987). *Patterns of attachment: A psychological study of the strange situation.* Psychology Press.

Barker, J. E., Semenov, A. D., Michaelson, L., Provan, L. S., Snyder, H. R., & Munakata, Y. (2014). Less-structured time in children's daily lives predicts self-directed executive functioning. *Frontiers in Psychology, 5,* 593. https://doi10.3389/fpsyg.2014.00593

Bartlett, J. D., Smith, S., & Bringewatt, E. (2017). *Helping young children who have experienced trauma: Policies and strategies for early care and education* (NCCP Publication No. 2017–19). National Center for Children in Poverty. https://www.childtrends.org/publications/ecetrauma

Barton, G., & Garvis, S. (2019). *Compassion and empathy in educational contexts.* Palgrave Macmillan.

Beebe, B., & Steele, M. (2013). How does microanalysis of mother–infant communication inform maternal sensitivity and infant attachment? *Attachment & Human Development, 15*(5–6), 583–602. https://doi.org/10.1080/14616734.2013.841050

Blachly, M., & Dean, N. (2019). *Feelings charts instead of behavior charts: Radical love instead of shame.* Ethics in Education. https://educate.bankstreet.edu/gse/1

Borntrager, C., Caringi, J. C., van den Pol, R., Crosby, L., O'Connell, K., Trautman, A., & McDonald, M. (2012). Secondary traumatic stress in school personnel. *Advances in School Mental Health Promotion, 5*(1), 38–50. https://doi.org/10.1080/1754730X.2012.664862

Bouie, J. (2020, July 31). John Lewis was the anti-Trump. *The New York Times,* Sunday Review.

Brickley, M., & Guyton, G. (2015). ACEs in early childhood teachers: An urban and rural sample. Unpublished manuscript from faculty study, Bank Street College.

Brown v. Board of Education of Topeka (1). (n.d.). Oyez. Retrieved August 27, 2020, from https://www.oyez.org/cases/1940-1955/347us483

Capistrano, C. G., Bianco, H., & Kim, P. (2016). Poverty and internalizing symptoms: The indirect effect of middle childhood poverty on internalizing symptoms via an emotional response inhibition pathway. *Frontiers in Psychology, 7, Article 1224*. https://doi.org/10.3389/fpsyg.2016.01242

Carver-Thomas, D., & Darling-Hammond, L. (2017). *Teacher turnover: Why it matters and what we can do about it*. Learning Policy Institute. https://learningpolicyinstitute.org/product/teacher-turnover

Chemakova, S. (2015). *Awkward*. Hachette Book Group.

Coleman, J. (2016). Racial differences in posttraumatic stress disorder in military personnel: Intergenerational transmission of trauma as a theoretical lens. *Journal of Aggression, Maltreatment and Trauma, 25*(6), 561–579. doi:10.1080/10926771.2016.1157842

Cook, A., Spinazzola, J., Ford, J., Lanktree, C., Blaustein, M., Cloitre, M., De-Rosa, R., Hubbard, R., Kagan, R., Liautaud, J., Mallah, K., Olafson, E., & Van der Kolk, B. (2005). Complex trauma in children and adolescents. *Psychiatric Annals, 35*(5), 390–398.

Darling-Hammond, L., Flook, L., Cook-Harvey, C., Barron, B., & Osher D. (2020). Implications for educational practice of the science of learning and development. *Applied Developmental Science, 24*(2), 97–140. https://doi.org/10.1080/10888691.2018.1537791

Dewey, J. (2015). *Democracy and education: An introduction to the philosophy of education*. CreateSpace Independent Publishing Platform (Original work published in 1916).

Dynarski, S., Hyman, J., & Schanzenbach, D. W. (2011). Experimental evidence on the effect of childhood investment on postsecondary attainment and degree completion. *Journal of Policy Analysis and Management, 32*(4), 692–717. https://www.nber.org/papers/w17533

Elledge, L. C., Elledge, A. R., Newgent, R. A., & Cavell, T. A. (2016). Social risk and peer victimization in elementary school children: The protective role of teacher-student relationships. *Journal of Abnormal Psychology, 44*, 691–703. https://doi.org/10.1007/s10802-015-0074-z

Flaherty, L. T., & Osher, D. (2002). History of school-based mental health services in the United States. In M. D. Weist, S. W. Evans, & N. A. Lever (Eds.), *Handbook of school mental health advancing practice and research* (pp. 11–22). *Issues in Clinical Child Psychology*. https://doi.org/10.1007/978-0-387-73313-5_2

Gaffney, C. (2019). When schools cause trauma. *Teaching Tolerance*, Issue 62. https://www.tolerance.org/magazine/summer-2019/when-schools-cause-trauma

Galinsky, E. (1987). *The six stages of parenthood*. Addison-Wesley.

Gilliam, W. S. (2005). *Prekindergarteners left behind: Expulsion rates in state prekindergarten programs*. Foundation for Child Development. https://www.fcd-us.org/prekindergartners-left-behind-expulsion-rates-in-state-prekindergarten-programs

Gonzalez, N., Moll, L. C., & Amanti, C. (2005). *Funds of knowledge: Theorizing practices in households, communities, and classrooms.* Lawrence Erlbaum.

Grey, P. (2010, January 26). The decline of play and rise in children's mental disorders. *Psychology Today.* https://www.psychologytoday.com/us/blog/freedom-learn/201001/the-decline-play-and-rise-in-childrens-mental-disorders

Hagan, M. J., Hulette, A. C., & Lieberman, A. F. (2015). Symptoms of dissociation in a high-risk sample of young children exposed to interpersonal trauma: Prevalence, correlates, and contributors. *National Library of Medicine, 28*(3), 258–261. doi:10.1002/jts.22003

Hatfield, B. E., & Williford, A. P. (2016). Cortisol patterns for young children displaying disruptive behavior: Links to a teacher-child, relationship-focused intervention. *Prevention Science, 18,* 40–49. https://doi.org/10.1007/s11121-016-0693-9

Heckman, J. J., & Karapakula, G. (2019). Intergenerational and intragenerational externalities of the Perry preschool project. *NBER Working Paper No. 25889.* https://www.nber.org/papers/w25889

Heilig, J. V., Williams, A., & Jez, S. J. (2010). Inputs and student achievement. An analysis of lantina/o-serving urban elementary schools. *Association of Mexican American Educators Journal, 4*(1). https://journals.coehd.utsa.edu/index.php/AMAE/article/view/44/37

Henkes, K. (1990). *Julius baby of the world* (K. Henkes, Illus.). Greenwillow Books.

Henkes, K. (2000). *Wemberly worried* (K. Henkes, Illus.). Greenwillow Books.

Hertzman, C., & Boyce, T. (2010). How experience gets under the skin to create gradients in developmental health. *Annual Review of Public Health, 31,* 329–347. 10.1146/annurev.publhealth.012809.103538

Ingersoll, R., Merrill, E., Stuckey, D., & Collins, G. (2018). *Seven trends: The transformation of the teaching force.* CPRE Research Reports. http://repository.upenn.edu/cpre_researchreports/108

Jacobson, D. A. (2016). *Causes and effects of teacher burnout* (Publication No. 2835). [*Doctoral Dissertation, Walden University*]. Scholar Works. https://scholarworks.waldenu.edu/dissertations/2835

Jensen, E. (2019). *Poor students, rich teaching.* Solution Tree Press.

Jensen, S. K. G., Berens, A. E., & Nelson, C. A. (2017). Effects of poverty on interacting biological systems underlying child development. *Lancet Child Adolescent Health, 1*(3), 225–239. https://doi.org/10.1016/S2352-4642(17)30024-X

Knoester, M., & Meier, D. (2017). *Beyond testing: Seven assessments of students and schools more effective than standardized tests.* Teachers College Press.

Konstantopoulos, S., & Chun, V. (2009). What are the long-term effects of small classes on the achievement gap? Evidence from the lasting benefits study. *American Journal of Education, 116*(1), 125–154. doi:10.1086/605103

Koplow, L. (2002). *Creating schools that heal: Real-life solutions.* Teachers College Press.

Koplow, L. (2007). *Unsmiling faces: How preschools can heal.* Teachers College Press.

Koplow, L. (2008). *Bears bears everywhere! Supporting children's emotional health in the classroom.* Teachers College Press.

Laínez, R. C. (2019). *My shoes and I: Crossing three boarders.* Mis zapatos y yo: cruzando tres fronteras (F. V. Broeck, Illus.). Piñata Books.

Lewis, J. (2020, July 30). Together, you can redeem the soul of our nation. *The New York Times, opinion pages.*

Lieberman, A., Zeanah, C., & McIntosh, J. (2011). Attachment perspectives on domestic violence and family law. *Family Court Review, 49*(3), 529–538. https://doi.org/10.1111/j.1744-1617.2011.01390.x

Mahler, M., Pine, F., & Bergman, A. (1985/2018). *The psychological birth of the human infant.* Routledge Press.

Mardell, B., Boni, M., & Sachs, J. (2013). Vivian Paley's storytelling/story acting comes to the Boston public schools. *Spotlight on young children, exploring language and literacy.* NAEYC. Editor, A. Shillady.

McInerney, M., & McKlindon, A. (2014). *Unlocking the door to learning: Trauma-informed classrooms & transformational schools. Education Law Center.* https://www.elc-pa.org/resource/unlocking-the-door-to-learning-trauma-informed-classrooms-and-transformational-schools

Miller, J. (1943/2010). *The whole child.* University of Toronto Press, Scholarly Publishing Division.

Mondale, S., & Patton, S. B. (2001). *School: The story of American public education.* Beacon Press.

NAACP. (2016). *NAACP plan of action for charter schools.* http://www.naacp.org/campaigns/naacp-plan-action-charter-schools

National Academies of Sciences, Engineering, and Medicine. (2020). *Promoting positive adolescent health behaviors and outcomes: Thriving in the 21st century.* National Academies Press. https://doi.org/10.17226/25552

National Commission on Excellence in Education. (1983). *A nation at risk.* https://www.maa.org/sites/default/files/pdf/CUPM/first_40years/1983-Risk.pdf

National Governors Association Center for Best Practices. (2010). *Common core state standards.* National Governors Association Center for Best Practices, Council of Chief State School Officers, Washington, DC.

National Scientific Council on the Developing Child. (2005). *Excessive stress disrupts the architecture of the developing brain. Working Paper No. 3.* Retrieved October 1, 2008, from http://www.developingchild.net/reports

National Scientific Council on the Developing Child. (2010a). *Early experiences can alter gene expression and affect long-term development. Working Paper No. 10.* www.developingchild.harvard.edu

National Scientific Council on the Developing Child. (2010b). *Persistent fear and anxiety can affect young children's learning and development. Working Paper No. 9.* https://46y5eh11fhgw3ve3ytpwxt9r-wpengine.netdna-ssl

.com/wp-content/uploads/2010/05/Persistent-Fear-and-Anxiety-Can
-Affect-Young-Childrens-Learning-and-Development.pdf

National Scientific Council on the Developing Child. (2012). *The science of neglect: The persistent absence of responsive care disrupts the developing brain. Working Paper No. 12*. https://46y5eh11fhgw3ve3ytpwxt9r-wpengine.netdna-ssl.com/wp-content/uploads/2012/05/The-Science-of-Neglect-The-Persistent-Absence-of-Responsive-Care-Disrupts-the-Developing-Brain.pdf

National Scientific Council on the Developing Child. (2015). *Supportive relationships and active skill-building strengthen the foundations of resilience. Working Paper No. 13*. https://46y5eh11fhgw3ve3ytpwxt9r-wpengine.netdna-ssl.com/wp-content/uploads/2015/05/The-Science-of-Resilience2.pdf

National Scientific Council on the Developing Child. (2018). *Understanding motivation: Building the brain architecture that supports learning, health, and community participation. Working Paper No. 14*. www.developingchild.harvard.edu

National Scientific Council on the Developing Child. (2020). *Connecting the brain to the rest of the body: Early childhood development and lifelong health are deeply intertwined. Working Paper No. 15*. https://46y5eh11fhgw3ve3ytpwxt9r-wpengine.netdna-ssl.com/wp-content/uploads/2020/06/wp15_health_FINAL.pdf.

Owens, M. T., & Tanner, K. D. (2017). Teaching as brain changing: Exploring connections between neuroscience and innovative teaching. *CBE Life Sciences Education, 16*(2). https://doi.org/10.1187/cbe.17-01-000510.1187/cbe.17-01-0005

Paley, V. G. (1991). *The boy who would be a helicopter: The use of storytelling in the classroom*. Harvard University Press.

Perry, B. D. (2000). Traumatized children: How childhood trauma influences brain development. *The Journal of the California Alliance for the Mentally Ill, 11*(1), 48–51. https://yourexperiencesmatter.com/resource/traumatized-children-how-childhood-trauma-influences-brain-development

Petchtel, P., & Pizzagalli, D. (2011). Effects of early life stress on cognitive and affective function: An integrated review of human literature. *Psychopharmacology, 214*(1), 55–70. https://doi.org/10.1007/s00213-010-2009-2

Powers et al. (2020). Intergenerational transmission of risk for PTSD symptoms in African American children: The roles of maternal and child emotional dysregulation. *Psychological trauma: Theory, research, practice and policy*. https://doi.org/10.1037/tra0000543

Ravitch, D. (2020). *Slaying goliath. The passionate resistance to privatization and the fight to save America's public*. Penguin Books.

Rawlings, W. K. (1992). *Friendship matters*. Routledge.

Reardon, S. F., Weathers, E., Fahle, E., Jang, H., & Kalogrides, D. (2020). Is separate still unequal? New evidence on school segregation and racial academic achievement gap. *CEPA Working Paper No. 19–06*. http://cepa.stanford.edu/wp19-06

Roorda, D., Koomna, H. M. Y., Split, J. L., & Oort, F. J. (2011). The influence of affective teacher-student relationships on student's school engagement and achievement. A meta-analytic approach. *Review of Educational Research, 81*(4), 493–529. doi:10.3102/0034654311421793

Sacks, V., & Murphy, D. (2018*). The prevalence of adverse childhood experiences, nationally, by state, and by race or ethnicity.* Child Trends. https://www.childtrends.org/publications/prevalence-adverse-childhood-experiences-nationally-state-race-ethnicity

Sahlberg, P. (2015). *Finnish lessons 2.0.* Teachers College Press.

Schiffrin, H. H., Godfrey, H., Liss, M., & Erchll, M. (2015). Intensive parenting: Does it have the desired impact on child outcomes? *Journal of Child and Family Studies, 24,* 2322–2331. https://doi.org/10.1007/s10826-014-0035-0

Schweinhardt, L. J., Barnes, H. V., & Weikart, D. P. (1993). *Significant benefits: The High-Scope Perry preschool study through age 27.* High Scope Press.

Shonkoff, J. (2019, February 7). Migrant family separation congressional testimony. Congress of the United States, Committee on Energy and Commerce, Subcommittee on Oversight and Investigations. Hearing on "Examining the failures of the Trump Administration's Inhumane Family Separation Policy."

Shonkoff, J., & Garner, A. (2011). The lifelong effects of early childhood adversity and toxic stress. *Pediatrics, 129*(1). https://doi.org/10.1542/peds.2011-2663

Sigman, A. (2019). A movement for movement. Screen time, physical activity, and sleep: A new integrated approach for children. *API supporting the UK play industry.* https://www.api-play.org/wp-content/uploads/sites/4/2019/01/API-Report-A-Movement-for-Movement-A4FINALWEB.pdf

Spilt, J. L., Leflot, G., & Colpin, H. (2019). Teacher involvement prevents increases in children's depressive symptoms: Bidirectional associations in elementary school. *Journal of Abnormal Psychology, 47*(2), 359–367. https://doi.org/10.1007/s10802-018-0441-7

Stearns, C. Z. (2019). *Critiquing social and emotional learning: Psychodynamic and cultural perspectives.* Lexington Books.

Stearns, P. N., & Stearns, C. Z. (1985). Emotionology: Clarifying the history of emotions and emotional standards. *The American Historical Review, 90*(4), 813–836. https://doi.org/10.1086/ahr/90.4.813

Stevens, C. (2020). "Tell me where it hurts": A case study of the impacts of structural violence, syndic suffering, and intergenerational trauma on indigenous people's health. In *Health matters: Evidence, critical social science and health care in Canada.* University of Toronto Press, Scholarly Publishing Division.

Substance Abuse and Mental Health Services Administration. (2014). *SAMHSA concept of trauma and guidance for a trauma-informed approach.* HHS Publication. No. (SMA) 14–4884.

Terr, L. (1992). *Too scared to cry: Psychic trauma in childhood.* Basic Books.

Terr, L., Bloch, D. A., Michel, B. A., Shi, H., Reinhardt, J. A., & Metayer, S. (1999). Children's symptoms in the wake of the challenger: A field study of distant traumatic effects and an outline of related conditions. *American Journal of Psychiatry, 156,* 1536–1544. https://ajp.psychiatryonline.org /doi/pdf/10.1176/ajp.156.10.1536

Thibodeau, R., Gilpin, A., Brown, M., & Meyer, B. (2016). The effects of fantastical pretend-play on the development of executive functions: An intervention study. *Journal of Experimental Child Psychology, 145,* 120–138. https://doi.org/10.1016/j.jecp.2016.01.001

Tierney, A. L., & Nelson, C. A. (2009). Brain development and the role of experience in the early years. *Zero to Three, 30*(2), 9–13.

Van der Kolk, B. A. (2000). Posttraumatic stress disorder and the nature of trauma. *Dialogues in Clinical Neuroscience, 2*(1), 7–22.

Van der Kolk, B. A. (2003). The neurobiology of childhood trauma and abuse. *Child & Adolescent Psychiatric Clinics, 12,* 293–317.

Van der Kolk, B. A. (2015). *The body keeps the score: Brain, mind, and body in the healing of trauma.* Viking Press.

Vygotsky, L. S. (1980). *Mind in society: The development of higher psychological processes.* Harvard University Press.

Weikart, D. P. (1987). *The Ypsilanti Perry preschool project: Preschool years and longitudinal results through fourth grade.* High/Scope Educational Research Foundation.

Wong, A. (2019, March 5). The schools that tried—but failed—to make Native Americans obsolete. *The Atlantic.* https://www.theatlantic.com/education /archive/2019/03/failed-assimilation-native-american-boarding-schools /584017

Wright, T. (2014). Too scared to learn: Teaching young children who have experienced trauma. *Young Children, 69*(5): 88–93.

Yogman, M., Garner, A., Hutchinson, J., Hirsh-Pasek, K., & Golinkoff, R. M. (2018). The power of play: A pediatric role in enhancing development in young children. *Pediatrics, 143*(3). https://doi.org/10.1542/peds.2018 -2058

Zulfiqar, N., Casale-Crouch, J., Sweeney, B., DeCoster, J., Rudasill, K. M., McGinnis, C., Acar, I., & Miller, K. (2018). Transition practices and children's development during kindergarten: The role of close teacher-child relationships. In A. Mashburn, J. LoCasale-Crouch, & K. Pears (Eds.), *Kindergarten transition and readiness.* Springer. https://doi.org/10.1007/978-3-319 -90200-5_12

Index

About the Author

Lesley Koplow, MS, LCSW, is the director of the Center for Emotionally Responsive Practice at Bank Street College in New York City, and the founder of Networks for Schools That Heal. She is the author of *Unsmiling Faces: How Preschools Can Heal, Creating Schools That Heal, Bears, Bears Everywhere: Supporting Children's Emotional Health in the Classroom*, as well as several other publications on supporting child mental health in schools.